Mometrix
TEST PREPARATION

CQI
Exam Secrets Study Guide

I0880299

DEAR FUTURE EXAM SUCCESS STORY

First of all, **THANK YOU** for purchasing Mometrix study materials!

Second, congratulations! You are one of the few determined test-takers who are committed to doing whatever it takes to excel on your exam. **You have come to the right place.** We developed these study materials with one goal in mind: to deliver you the information you need in a format that's concise and easy to use.

In addition to optimizing your guide for the content of the test, we've outlined our recommended steps for breaking down the preparation process into small, attainable goals so you can make sure you stay on track.

We've also analyzed the entire test-taking process, identifying the most common pitfalls and showing how you can overcome them and be ready for any curveball the test throws you.

Standardized testing is one of the biggest obstacles on your road to success, which only increases the importance of doing well in the high-pressure, high-stakes environment of test day. Your results on this test could have a significant impact on your future, and this guide provides the information and practical advice to help you achieve your full potential on test day.

Your success is our success

We would love to hear from you! If you would like to share the story of your exam success or if you have any questions or comments in regard to our products, please contact us at **800-673-8175** or **support@mometrix.com**.

Thanks again for your business and we wish you continued success!

Sincerely,
The Mometrix Test Preparation Team

Need more help? Check out our flashcards at:
http://MometrixFlashcards.com/CQI

Written and edited by the Mometrix Exam Secrets Test Prep Team
Printed in the United States of America

TABLE OF CONTENTS

Introduction

Thank you for purchasing this resource! You have made the choice to prepare yourself for a test that could have a huge impact on your future, and this guide is designed to help you be fully ready for test day. Obviously, it's important to have a solid understanding of the test material, but you also need to be prepared for the unique environment and stressors of the test, so that you can perform to the best of your abilities.

For this purpose, the first section that appears in this guide is the **Secret Keys**. We've devoted countless hours to meticulously researching what works and what doesn't, and we've boiled down our findings to the five most impactful steps you can take to improve your performance on the test. We start at the beginning with study planning and move through the preparation process, all the way to the testing strategies that will help you get the most out of what you know when you're finally sitting in front of the test.

We recommend that you start preparing for your test as far in advance as possible. However, if you've bought this guide as a last-minute study resource and only have a few days before your test, we recommend that you skip over the first two Secret Keys since they address a long-term study plan.

If you struggle with **test anxiety**, we strongly encourage you to check out our recommendations for how you can overcome it. Test anxiety is a formidable foe, but it can be beaten, and we want to make sure you have the tools you need to defeat it.

Secret Key #1 – Plan Big, Study Small

There's a lot riding on your performance. If you want to ace this test, you're going to need to keep your skills sharp and the material fresh in your mind. You need a plan that lets you review everything you need to know while still fitting in your schedule. We'll break this strategy down into three categories.

Information Organization

Start with the information you already have: the official test outline. From this, you can make a complete list of all the concepts you need to cover before the test. Organize these concepts into groups that can be studied together, and create a list of any related vocabulary you need to learn so you can brush up on any difficult terms. You'll want to keep this vocabulary list handy once you actually start studying since you may need to add to it along the way.

Time Management

Once you have your set of study concepts, decide how to spread them out over the time you have left before the test. Break your study plan into small, clear goals so you have a manageable task for each day and know exactly what you're doing. Then just focus on one small step at a time. When you manage your time this way, you don't need to spend hours at a time studying. Studying a small block of content for a short period each day helps you retain information better and avoid stressing over how much you have left to do. You can relax knowing that you have a plan to cover everything in time. In order for this strategy to be effective though, you have to start studying early and stick to your schedule. Avoid the exhaustion and futility that comes from last-minute cramming!

Study Environment

The environment you study in has a big impact on your learning. Studying in a coffee shop, while probably more enjoyable, is not likely to be as fruitful as studying in a quiet room. It's important to keep distractions to a minimum. You're only planning to study for a short block of time, so make the most of it. Don't pause to check your phone or get up to find a snack. It's also important to **avoid multitasking**. Research has consistently shown that multitasking will make your studying dramatically less effective. Your study area should also be comfortable and well-lit so you don't have the distraction of straining your eyes or sitting on an uncomfortable chair.

The time of day you study is also important. You want to be rested and alert. Don't wait until just before bedtime. Study when you'll be most likely to comprehend and remember. Even better, if you know what time of day your test will be, set that time aside for study. That way your brain will be used to working on that subject at that specific time and you'll have a better chance of recalling information.

Finally, it can be helpful to team up with others who are studying for the same test. Your actual studying should be done in as isolated an environment as possible, but the work of organizing the information and setting up the study plan can be divided up. In between study sessions, you can discuss with your teammates the concepts that you're all studying and quiz each other on the details. Just be sure that your teammates are as serious about the test as you are. If you find that your study time is being replaced with social time, you might need to find a new team.

Secret Key #2 – Make Your Studying Count

You're devoting a lot of time and effort to preparing for this test, so you want to be absolutely certain it will pay off. This means doing more than just reading the content and hoping you can remember it on test day. It's important to make every minute of study count. There are two main areas you can focus on to make your studying count.

Retention

It doesn't matter how much time you study if you can't remember the material. You need to make sure you are retaining the concepts. To check your retention of the information you're learning, try recalling it at later times with minimal prompting. Try carrying around flashcards and glance at one or two from time to time or ask a friend who's also studying for the test to quiz you.

To enhance your retention, look for ways to put the information into practice so that you can apply it rather than simply recalling it. If you're using the information in practical ways, it will be much easier to remember. Similarly, it helps to solidify a concept in your mind if you're not only reading it to yourself but also explaining it to someone else. Ask a friend to let you teach them about a concept you're a little shaky on (or speak aloud to an imaginary audience if necessary). As you try to summarize, define, give examples, and answer your friend's questions, you'll understand the concepts better and they will stay with you longer. Finally, step back for a big picture view and ask yourself how each piece of information fits with the whole subject. When you link the different concepts together and see them working together as a whole, it's easier to remember the individual components.

Finally, practice showing your work on any multi-step problems, even if you're just studying. Writing out each step you take to solve a problem will help solidify the process in your mind, and you'll be more likely to remember it during the test.

Modality

Modality simply refers to the means or method by which you study. Choosing a study modality that fits your own individual learning style is crucial. No two people learn best in exactly the same way, so it's important to know your strengths and use them to your advantage.

For example, if you learn best by visualization, focus on visualizing a concept in your mind and draw an image or a diagram. Try color-coding your notes, illustrating them, or creating symbols that will trigger your mind to recall a learned concept. If you learn best by hearing or discussing information, find a study partner who learns the same way or read aloud to yourself. Think about how to put the information in your own words. Imagine that you are giving a lecture on the topic and record yourself so you can listen to it later.

For any learning style, flashcards can be helpful. Organize the information so you can take advantage of spare moments to review. Underline key words or phrases. Use different colors for different categories. Mnemonic devices (such as creating a short list in which every item starts with the same letter) can also help with retention. Find what works best for you and use it to store the information in your mind most effectively and easily.

Secret Key #3 – Practice the Right Way

Your success on test day depends not only on how many hours you put into preparing, but also on whether you prepared the right way. It's good to check along the way to see if your studying is paying off. One of the most effective ways to do this is by taking practice tests to evaluate your progress. Practice tests are useful because they show exactly where you need to improve. Every time you take a practice test, pay special attention to these three groups of questions:

- The questions you got wrong
- The questions you had to guess on, even if you guessed right
- The questions you found difficult or slow to work through

This will show you exactly what your weak areas are, and where you need to devote more study time. Ask yourself why each of these questions gave you trouble. Was it because you didn't understand the material? Was it because you didn't remember the vocabulary? Do you need more repetitions on this type of question to build speed and confidence? Dig into those questions and figure out how you can strengthen your weak areas as you go back to review the material.

Additionally, many practice tests have a section explaining the answer choices. It can be tempting to read the explanation and think that you now have a good understanding of the concept. However, an explanation likely only covers part of the question's broader context. Even if the explanation makes perfect sense, **go back and investigate** every concept related to the question until you're positive you have a thorough understanding.

As you go along, keep in mind that the practice test is just that: practice. Memorizing these questions and answers will not be very helpful on the actual test because it is unlikely to have any of the same exact questions. If you only know the right answers to the sample questions, you won't be prepared for the real thing. **Study the concepts** until you understand them fully, and then you'll be able to answer any question that shows up on the test.

It's important to wait on the practice tests until you're ready. If you take a test on your first day of study, you may be overwhelmed by the amount of material covered and how much you need to learn. Work up to it gradually.

On test day, you'll need to be prepared for answering questions, managing your time, and using the test-taking strategies you've learned. It's a lot to balance, like a mental marathon that will have a big impact on your future. Like training for a marathon, you'll need to start slowly and work your way up. When test day arrives, you'll be ready.

Start with the strategies you've read in the first two Secret Keys—plan your course and study in the way that works best for you. If you have time, consider using multiple study resources to get different approaches to the same concepts. It can be helpful to see difficult concepts from more than one angle. Then find a good source for practice tests. Many times, the test website will suggest potential study resources or provide sample tests.

Practice Test Strategy

If you're able to find at least three practice tests, we recommend this strategy:

Untimed and Open-Book Practice

Take the first test with no time constraints and with your notes and study guide handy. Take your time and focus on applying the strategies you've learned.

Timed and Open-Book Practice

Take the second practice test open-book as well, but set a timer and practice pacing yourself to finish in time.

Timed and Closed-Book Practice

Take any other practice tests as if it were test day. Set a timer and put away your study materials. Sit at a table or desk in a quiet room, imagine yourself at the testing center, and answer questions as quickly and accurately as possible.

Keep repeating timed and closed-book tests on a regular basis until you run out of practice tests or it's time for the actual test. Your mind will be ready for the schedule and stress of test day, and you'll be able to focus on recalling the material you've learned.

Secret Key #4 – Pace Yourself

Once you're fully prepared for the material on the test, your biggest challenge on test day will be managing your time. Just knowing that the clock is ticking can make you panic even if you have plenty of time left. Work on pacing yourself so you can build confidence against the time constraints of the exam. Pacing is a difficult skill to master, especially in a high-pressure environment, so **practice is vital**.

Set time expectations for your pace based on how much time is available. For example, if a section has 60 questions and the time limit is 30 minutes, you know you have to average 30 seconds or less per question in order to answer them all. Although 30 seconds is the hard limit, set 25 seconds per question as your goal, so you reserve extra time to spend on harder questions. When you budget extra time for the harder questions, you no longer have any reason to stress when those questions take longer to answer.

Don't let this time expectation distract you from working through the test at a calm, steady pace, but keep it in mind so you don't spend too much time on any one question. Recognize that taking extra time on one question you don't understand may keep you from answering two that you do understand later in the test. If your time limit for a question is up and you're still not sure of the answer, mark it and move on, and come back to it later if the time and the test format allow. If the testing format doesn't allow you to return to earlier questions, just make an educated guess; then put it out of your mind and move on.

On the easier questions, be careful not to rush. It may seem wise to hurry through them so you have more time for the challenging ones, but it's not worth missing one if you know the concept and just didn't take the time to read the question fully. Work efficiently but make sure you understand the question and have looked at all of the answer choices, since more than one may seem right at first.

Even if you're paying attention to the time, you may find yourself a little behind at some point. You should speed up to get back on track, but do so wisely. Don't panic; just take a few seconds less on each question until you're caught up. Don't guess without thinking, but do look through the answer choices and eliminate any you know are wrong. If you can get down to two choices, it is often worthwhile to guess from those. Once you've chosen an answer, move on and don't dwell on any that you skipped or had to hurry through. If a question was taking too long, chances are it was one of the harder ones, so you weren't as likely to get it right anyway.

On the other hand, if you find yourself getting ahead of schedule, it may be beneficial to slow down a little. The more quickly you work, the more likely you are to make a careless mistake that will affect your score. You've budgeted time for each question, so don't be afraid to spend that time. Practice an efficient but careful pace to get the most out of the time you have.

Secret Key #5 – Have a Plan for Guessing

When you're taking the test, you may find yourself stuck on a question. Some of the answer choices seem better than others, but you don't see the one answer choice that is obviously correct. What do you do?

The scenario described above is very common, yet most test takers have not effectively prepared for it. Developing and practicing a plan for guessing may be one of the single most effective uses of your time as you get ready for the exam.

In developing your plan for guessing, there are three questions to address:

- When should you start the guessing process?
- How should you narrow down the choices?
- Which answer should you choose?

When to Start the Guessing Process

Unless your plan for guessing is to select C every time (which, despite its merits, is not what we recommend), you need to leave yourself enough time to apply your answer elimination strategies. Since you have a limited amount of time for each question, that means that if you're going to give yourself the best shot at guessing correctly, you have to decide quickly whether or not you will guess.

Of course, the best-case scenario is that you don't have to guess at all, so first, see if you can answer the question based on your knowledge of the subject and basic reasoning skills. Focus on the key words in the question and try to jog your memory of related topics. Give yourself a chance to bring the knowledge to mind, but once you realize that you don't have (or you can't access) the knowledge you need to answer the question, it's time to start the guessing process.

It's almost always better to start the guessing process too early than too late. It only takes a few seconds to remember something and answer the question from knowledge. Carefully eliminating wrong answer choices takes longer. Plus, going through the process of eliminating answer choices can actually help jog your memory.

Summary: Start the guessing process as soon as you decide that you can't answer the question based on your knowledge.

How to Narrow Down the Choices

The next chapter in this book (**Test-Taking Strategies**) includes a wide range of strategies for how to approach questions and how to look for answer choices to eliminate. You will definitely want to read those carefully, practice them, and figure out which ones work best for you. Here though, we're going to address a mindset rather than a particular strategy.

Your odds of guessing an answer correctly depend on how many options you are choosing from.

Number of options left	5	4	3	2	1
Odds of guessing correctly	20%	25%	33%	50%	100%

You can see from this chart just how valuable it is to be able to eliminate incorrect answers and make an educated guess, but there are two things that many test takers do that cause them to miss out on the benefits of guessing:

- Accidentally eliminating the correct answer
- Selecting an answer based on an impression

We'll look at the first one here, and the second one in the next section.

To avoid accidentally eliminating the correct answer, we recommend a thought exercise called **the $5 challenge**. In this challenge, you only eliminate an answer choice from contention if you are willing to bet $5 on it being wrong. Why $5? Five dollars is a small but not insignificant amount of money. It's an amount you could afford to lose but wouldn't want to throw away. And while losing $5 once might not hurt too much, doing it twenty times will set you back $100. In the same way, each small decision you make—eliminating a choice here, guessing on a question there—won't by itself impact your score very much, but when you put them all together, they can make a big difference. By holding each answer choice elimination decision to a higher standard, you can reduce the risk of accidentally eliminating the correct answer.

The $5 challenge can also be applied in a positive sense: If you are willing to bet $5 that an answer choice *is* correct, go ahead and mark it as correct.

Summary: Only eliminate an answer choice if you are willing to bet $5 that it is wrong.

Which Answer to Choose

You're taking the test. You've run into a hard question and decided you'll have to guess. You've eliminated all the answer choices you're willing to bet $5 on. Now you have to pick an answer. Why do we even need to talk about this? Why can't you just pick whichever one you feel like when the time comes?

The answer to these questions is that if you don't come into the test with a plan, you'll rely on your impression to select an answer choice, and if you do that, you risk falling into a trap. The test writers know that everyone who takes their test will be guessing on some of the questions, so they intentionally write wrong answer choices to seem plausible. You still have to pick an answer though, and if the wrong answer choices are designed to look right, how can you ever be sure that you're not falling for their trap? The best solution we've found to this dilemma is to take the decision out of your hands entirely. Here is the process we recommend:

Once you've eliminated any choices that you are confident (willing to bet $5) are wrong, select the first remaining choice as your answer.

Whether you choose to select the first remaining choice, the second, or the last, the important thing is that you use some preselected standard. Using this approach guarantees that you will not be enticed into selecting an answer choice that looks right, because you are not basing your decision on how the answer choices look.

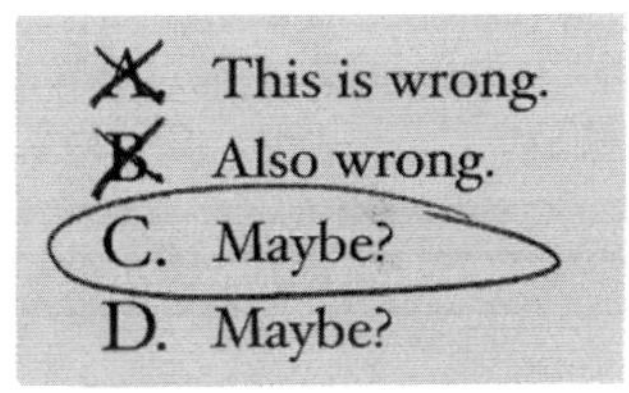

This is not meant to make you question your knowledge. Instead, it is to help you recognize the difference between your knowledge and your impressions. There's a huge difference between thinking an answer is right because of what you know, and thinking an answer is right because it looks or sounds like it should be right.

Summary: To ensure that your selection is appropriately random, make a predetermined selection from among all answer choices you have not eliminated.

Test-Taking Strategies

This section contains a list of test-taking strategies that you may find helpful as you work through the test. By taking what you know and applying logical thought, you can maximize your chances of answering any question correctly!

It is very important to realize that every question is different and every person is different: no single strategy will work on every question, and no single strategy will work for every person. That's why we've included all of them here, so you can try them out and determine which ones work best for different types of questions and which ones work best for you.

Question Strategies

✓ Read Carefully

Read the question and the answer choices carefully. Don't miss the question because you misread the terms. You have plenty of time to read each question thoroughly and make sure you understand what is being asked. Yet a happy medium must be attained, so don't waste too much time. You must read carefully and efficiently.

✓ Contextual Clues

Look for contextual clues. If the question includes a word you are not familiar with, look at the immediate context for some indication of what the word might mean. Contextual clues can often give you all the information you need to decipher the meaning of an unfamiliar word. Even if you can't determine the meaning, you may be able to narrow down the possibilities enough to make a solid guess at the answer to the question.

✓ Prefixes

If you're having trouble with a word in the question or answer choices, try dissecting it. Take advantage of every clue that the word might include. Prefixes can be a huge help. Usually, they allow you to determine a basic meaning. *Pre-* means before, *post-* means after, *pro-* is positive, *de-* is negative. From prefixes, you can get an idea of the general meaning of the word and try to put it into context.

✓ Hedge Words

Watch out for critical hedge words, such as *likely, may, can, often, almost, mostly, usually, generally, rarely*, and *sometimes*. Question writers insert these hedge phrases to cover every possibility. Often an answer choice will be wrong simply because it leaves no room for exception. Be on guard for answer choices that have definitive words such as *exactly* and *always*.

✓ Switchback Words

Stay alert for *switchbacks*. These are the words and phrases frequently used to alert you to shifts in thought. The most common switchback words are *but, although*, and *however*. Others include *nevertheless, on the other hand, even though, while, in spite of, despite*, and *regardless of*. Switchback words are important to catch because they can change the direction of the question or an answer choice.

✓ Face Value

When in doubt, use common sense. Accept the situation in the problem at face value. Don't read too much into it. These problems will not require you to make wild assumptions. If you have to go beyond creativity and warp time or space in order to have an answer choice fit the question, then you should move on and consider the other answer choices. These are normal problems rooted in reality. The applicable relationship or explanation may not be readily apparent, but it is there for you to figure out. Use your common sense to interpret anything that isn't clear.

Answer Choice Strategies

✓ Answer Selection

The most thorough way to pick an answer choice is to identify and eliminate wrong answers until only one is left, then confirm it is the correct answer. Sometimes an answer choice may immediately seem right, but be careful. The test writers will usually put more than one reasonable answer choice on each question, so take a second to read all of them and make sure that the other choices are not equally obvious. As long as you have time left, it is better to read every answer choice than to pick the first one that looks right without checking the others.

✓ Answer Choice Families

An answer choice family consists of two (in rare cases, three) answer choices that are very similar in construction and cannot all be true at the same time. If you see two answer choices that are direct opposites or parallels, one of them is usually the correct answer. For instance, if one answer choice says that quantity *x* increases and another either says that quantity *x* decreases (opposite) or says that quantity *y* increases (parallel), then those answer choices would fall into the same family. An answer choice that doesn't match the construction of the answer choice family is more likely to be incorrect. Most questions will not have answer choice families, but when they do appear, you should be prepared to recognize them.

✓ Eliminate Answers

Eliminate answer choices as soon as you realize they are wrong, but make sure you consider all possibilities. If you are eliminating answer choices and realize that the last one you are left with is also wrong, don't panic. Start over and consider each choice again. There may be something you missed the first time that you will realize on the second pass.

✓ Avoid Fact Traps

Don't be distracted by an answer choice that is factually true but doesn't answer the question. You are looking for the choice that answers the question. Stay focused on what the question is asking for so you don't accidentally pick an answer that is true but incorrect. Always go back to the question and make sure the answer choice you've selected actually answers the question and is not merely a true statement.

✓ Extreme Statements

In general, you should avoid answers that put forth extreme actions as standard practice or proclaim controversial ideas as established fact. An answer choice that states the "process should be used in certain situations, if..." is much more likely to be correct than one that states the "process should be discontinued completely." The first is a calm rational statement and doesn't even make a definitive, uncompromising stance, using a hedge word *if* to provide wiggle room, whereas the second choice is far more extreme.

⊘ Benchmark

As you read through the answer choices and you come across one that seems to answer the question well, mentally select that answer choice. This is not your final answer, but it's the one that will help you evaluate the other answer choices. The one that you selected is your benchmark or standard for judging each of the other answer choices. Every other answer choice must be compared to your benchmark. That choice is correct until proven otherwise by another answer choice beating it. If you find a better answer, then that one becomes your new benchmark. Once you've decided that no other choice answers the question as well as your benchmark, you have your final answer.

⊘ Predict the Answer

Before you even start looking at the answer choices, it is often best to try to predict the answer. When you come up with the answer on your own, it is easier to avoid distractions and traps because you will know exactly what to look for. The right answer choice is unlikely to be word-for-word what you came up with, but it should be a close match. Even if you are confident that you have the right answer, you should still take the time to read each option before moving on.

General Strategies

⊘ Tough Questions

If you are stumped on a problem or it appears too hard or too difficult, don't waste time. Move on! Remember though, if you can quickly check for obviously incorrect answer choices, your chances of guessing correctly are greatly improved. Before you completely give up, at least try to knock out a couple of possible answers. Eliminate what you can and then guess at the remaining answer choices before moving on.

⊘ Check Your Work

Since you will probably not know every term listed and the answer to every question, it is important that you get credit for the ones that you do know. Don't miss any questions through careless mistakes. If at all possible, try to take a second to look back over your answer selection and make sure you've selected the correct answer choice and haven't made a costly careless mistake (such as marking an answer choice that you didn't mean to mark). This quick double check should more than pay for itself in caught mistakes for the time it costs.

⊘ Pace Yourself

It's easy to be overwhelmed when you're looking at a page full of questions; your mind is confused and full of random thoughts, and the clock is ticking down faster than you would like. Calm down and maintain the pace that you have set for yourself. Especially as you get down to the last few minutes of the test, don't let the small numbers on the clock make you panic. As long as you are on track by monitoring your pace, you are guaranteed to have time for each question.

⊘ Don't Rush

It is very easy to make errors when you are in a hurry. Maintaining a fast pace in answering questions is pointless if it makes you miss questions that you would have gotten right otherwise. Test writers like to include distracting information and wrong answers that seem right. Taking a little extra time to avoid careless mistakes can make all the difference in your test score. Find a pace that allows you to be confident in the answers that you select.

⊘ KEEP MOVING

Panicking will not help you pass the test, so do your best to stay calm and keep moving. Taking deep breaths and going through the answer elimination steps you practiced can help to break through a stress barrier and keep your pace.

Final Notes

The combination of a solid foundation of content knowledge and the confidence that comes from practicing your plan for applying that knowledge is the key to maximizing your performance on test day. As your foundation of content knowledge is built up and strengthened, you'll find that the strategies included in this chapter become more and more effective in helping you quickly sift through the distractions and traps of the test to isolate the correct answer.

Now that you're preparing to move forward into the test content chapters of this book, be sure to keep your goal in mind. As you read, think about how you will be able to apply this information on the test. If you've already seen sample questions for the test and you have an idea of the question format and style, try to come up with questions of your own that you can answer based on what you're reading. This will give you valuable practice applying your knowledge in the same ways you can expect to on test day.

Good luck and good studying!

Technical Mathematics

Significant Figures

Significant figures are generally an estimate of accuracy for a given measurement. The figures are usually determined either by the measuring instrument or a lower bound for measurement if given a set of values; e.g. if three values must be combined, and two of the values have five significant digits but one has three, then the result must be expressed to three significant figures. Significant figures can be counted in numerous ways, but in virtually all measurement applications, significant figures (or digits) are considered to be those after the decimal point. Additionally, depending on the accuracy and precision requirements, the significant figures can be arrived at through either truncation—chopping off whatever digits remain after the declared digit limit—or through rounding, where the value is adjusted downward (if the digits after the accuracy limit are 49 or lower) or upward (50 or higher).

First-Degree Equations

A first-degree equation is an equation in the form ax + by = c such that the variables x and y are expressed in the first power; that is, the variables are only a constant multiplier of themselves, not multiplied by itself some given number of times (i.e. x^2 or y^2). In these equations, either a or b can have a value of zero, but not both; negative values are possible for all constants. First-degree equations are most frequently used to determine the value of a given unknown value and to plot straight lines on a Cartesian, or two-dimensional, graph, where x is the horizontal component and the vertical component y is determined by manipulating the equation to determine the slope of the line (expressed as rise divided by run) and working backwards.

Single-Variable Equations

A single-variable equation is any equation that can be expressed as ax+b=c, such that a and c are constants. c can be equal to zero in this definition, but a must be non-zero. Single-variable equations and first-degree equations are very similar in construction and in their usage, although single-variable equations do not have the same exponential strictures that first-degree equations do; expressions such as $x^2 + 4x + 8 = 0$ would technically be considered single-variable since all variable terms are expressed in terms of x, although it is not a first-degree equation due to the presence of x^2. Generally, however, a single-variable equation will have only one variable term, with that variable being expressed in the first power.

Area

Area is a two-dimensional measure of the size of a given space, such as land surface or the outer shell of a container (if referring to the total outer layer of a three-dimensional object, surface area is used). Area is a measurement most commonly used to describe real estate. To determine the area of a given space or plot, the width and the depth of the space must be measured, and then multiplied to provide the total area in square units, e.g. ft^2 or mi^2. The general equation for determining area is A=wd, where w is the width of the space and d is the depth. For circular fields, area is determined by the formula $A=\pi r^2$, where r is the radius, or distance from the center to the edge, of the circle. Depending on the orientation of the space relative to the observer, height and breadth may also be used in area computation.

Volume

Volume, unlike area, is a three-dimensional measurement, specifically of the total space encompassed by an object. It can refer to displacement or capacity to hold. To determine the volume of a given space or solid, the width, height and depth of the space must be measured, and then multiplied to provide the total volume in cubed units, e.g. ft^3 or cm^3. The general equation for volume is V=w*h*d, where w is the width of the object or solid, h is the height and d is the depth. Different variants of this basic equation are used depending on the nature of the solid or space for which volume is being computed, but most can be derived from the essential definition.

Circumference

Circumference is the total distance around a circular space; as generally used, it is the term for perimeter when referring to circular spaces. It can also be thought of as the boundary limit for any closed curve. The general equation for circumference is $C=2\pi r$, where r is the radius, or distance from the center to the edge, of the circle; a simpler version is $C=d\pi$, where d is the diameter, which is any line that touches two points on the circle edge and passes through the center (2r is always equal to d in plane geometry). Circumference is a linear measurement, and is always given in first-degree regular units of measure, e.g. ft or m.

Perimeter

Perimeter is the total distance around the outer edge of a field or figure; circumference is essentially a special case of a perimeter. The basic method of determining the values of a perimeter is to add up all the line segments that make up the outer edge of a figure or field. With rectangular fields, the equation is $P=2x + 2y$, where x is the length of the longer side and y is the length of the shorter side; with square fields, the equation simplifies to $P=4x$, where x is simply the length of one side. Depending on the shape of the figure or field, the computation of the perimeter value can be lengthy, although not complicated.

Complementary Angles

Complementary angles are simply two angles that, when summed together, add up to make a right angle, or 90°. One example of complementary angles would be two angles measuring 45°, as 45 + 45 = 90; another example would be two angles measuring 37° and 53°, since 37 + 53 = 90. By definition, all complementary angles are acute, or less than 90°, since negative numbers are not used in measuring angles. Complementary angles have multiple uses in plane geometry and trigonometry, and in machining by extension, and can be used in conjunction with the Pythagorean theorem to help determine the size of triangular spaces where one angle is a right angle.

Supplementary Angles

Supplementary angles are a pair of angles that, when the measurements are summed together, add up to make 180°, which can be thought of as a semicircle or a straight line, depending on the shape of the problem the measurements are applied to by the user. One example of supplementary angles would be two angles measuring 90°, as 90 + 90 = 180; another example would be 62° and 118°, as 62 + 118 = 180. With a pair of supplementary angles, one angle will always be obtuse, or greater than 90°, and one angle will always be acute, or less than 90°, unless using the special case of two right angles.

Sine

Sine is a trigonometric function, or function of an angle, that defines the ratio of sides in a right triangle, or one that has a 90° angle. Specifically, the sine of an angle a is the ratio of the side directly opposite to the angle a to the hypotenuse of the triangle. Alternately, the sine of an angle can be seen as the length of a specific line taken from a circle with a radius of 1 unit, which is known as a unit circle. Due to the fact that all right triangles are considered similar, meaning that they share basic properties, numeric values for the sine of various angles can be determined regardless of the length of the triangle's sides.

Cosine

Cosine is a trigonometric function, or function of an angle, that defines the ratio of sides in a right triangle, or one that has a 90° angle. Specifically, the cosine of an angle a is the ratio of the side directly adjacent to the angle a to the hypotenuse of the triangle. Alternately, the cosine of an angle can be seen as the length of a specific line taken from a circle with a radius of 1 unit, which is known as a unit circle. Due to the fact that all right triangles are considered similar, meaning that they share basic properties, numeric values for the cosine of various angles can be determined regardless of the length of the triangle's sides.

Tangent

Tangent is a trigonometric function, or function of an angle, that defines the ratio of sides in a right triangle, or one that has a 90° angle. Specifically, the tangent of an angle a is the ratio of the side directly opposite to the angle a to the side directly opposite to the angle a; the tangent of angle a can thus be determined using the following equation: $\tan(a) = \sin(a)/\cos(a)$. Alternately, the tangent can be seen as a line which touches a given curve at only one singular point. Due to the fact that all right triangles are considered similar, meaning that they share basic properties, numeric values for the tangent of various angles can be determined regardless of the length of the triangle's sides, either independently of the other trigonometric functions or by using them directly.

Pythagorean Theorem

The Pythagorean theorem relates to the relationship between the sides of a right triangle. It is most commonly formulated as $c^2 = a^2 + b^2$, where c is the hypotenuse of the right triangle, and a and b are the remaining sides. Other trigonometric relationships can be derived using the Pythagorean theorem, but it is most commonly used to derive the sides of a triangle. For example, if you have a right triangle with a vertical side of length 5 inches and a horizontal side of 12 inches, you can determine the length of the hypotenuse by inserting the known values into the formula and getting $c^2 = (5)^2 + (12)^2$, which yields $c^2 = 25 + 144$, which simplifies to $c^2 = 169$, and by taking the square root of both sides, we see that $c = 13$, so the hypotenuse is 13 inches.

Hypotenuse

The hypotenuse is defined as the segment of a right triangle that is directly opposite the right angle. The hypotenuse is always the longest of the triangle's sides, and is generally defined as c in standard geometric notation. This standard is most commonly expressed in the standard form of the Pythagorean theorem, which is $c^2 = a^2 + b^2$. In most standard diagrams of right triangles, the hypotenuse is the diagonal segment that connects the endpoints of the vertical and horizontal segments. Alternately, the hypotenuse can be viewed as the common denominator in the definitions of sine and cosine, since both functions rely on the hypotenuse as part of their definitions.

SI Measurement System

The SI, which stands for Systeme International d'Unites, system is the globally accepted standard for measuring units in science, engineering and industrial fields. SI was developed in the 1960s, and is an updated version of the metric system. Its primary difference is that the base units of the SI system are meter (for length and distance), kilogram (for mass and weight), and second (for time), as well as other units measuring electrical current, luminosity and a few other physical measurements. The standard definitions for these units are in most cases the same as the metric system; although SI takes a different set for the base units, the units themselves are equivalent in nearly all cases.

English Measurement System

The English measurement system, also known as the American system since the USA is the only major nation to continue using this system, is based on the Imperial system that was developed in England over the centuries. The base units as commonly used are the foot, yard, and mile (for length or distance) and the second (time). A standardized mass measurement was never developed in a general sense; instead there were four mass systems that measured mass, weight and force: tower, which was never used in the United States, troy, avoirdupois, which is the primary measure of mass in the English system today, and apothecaries' system, which was only used in pharmacies.

Metric Measurement System

The metric measurement system, developed in France in the aftermath of the French Revolution, was an attempt to standardize measurements into one logical system. It is the predecessor of the SI system, and shares many of the same units and general definitions. Unlike the SI system, the metric system was based on physical prototypes, which were subject to imprecise measurements and physical changes in the base properties over time. Also unlike the SI system, several variants of the metric system developed over time, using different units as their bases, such as the centimeter-gram-second system that was one of the first conceptual frameworks for the system, or the meter-tonne-second system used in the Soviet Union for many years.

Unit Conversion

Unit conversion is the process of taking measurements made in one measurement system and, by using defined relationships, transforming those measurements into equivalent figures in another system. Transformations from metric to SI are frequently trivial, as most of the units and standards are identical for both systems, but unit conversions from English to SI or vice versa do not have straightforward transformations, and require attention; also, the exact transformations may use different figures, depending on the level of precision needed. In performing unit conversion, one must always know both the level of precision needed and the exact units the final result needs to be phrased in; e.g. converting feet to meters, yards to kilometers, ounces to grams, etc.

Square Roots

The square root of a number (denoted here as x) is simply a number r that when multiplied by itself, or "squared," yields x. Written in equation form, the square root r of x is such that r*r (or r^2) = x. There are several methods of computing square roots, including using the square root function on a standard calculator, but one of the simplest methods—and one that can be done by hand—is known as the Babylonian method. To determine the square root r of a number x using this method, start by taking any positive value less than x (estimating what the answer is likely to be may help in determining this value, but it is not necessary). Determine the average of the chosen value of r and x/r. Repeat the averaging as many times as needed for a given level of precision and accuracy.

Scientific Notation

Scientific notation is a method of expressing numbers in a logical and efficient fashion without creating unwieldy expressions of digits. Numbers are expressed using powers of 10 instead of writing out all the digits; for example, 1,000,000 in scientific notation is 1×10^6, or more simply, 10^6. In another example, 45,672,500 would be written as 4.56725×10^7; ending zeros do not need to be included in the full number, as their presence is indicated in the exponent. Accuracy and precision requirements often determine the full expression of the number being expressed, but the exponent piece of the expression should not be affected. Numbers less than 1 can also be expressed in scientific notation using negative exponents; .25, for example, can be expressed as 2.5×10^{-1}.

Decimals

The term decimal refers to the numeral system that is most commonly used by humans, as it is a base-10 system (meaning that every digit in a given number represents a power of ten). Common context of the term generally refers to either numbers that are a composite of whole numbers and pieces less than 1 concatenated into a numeric expression joined by a decimal point, e.g. 3994.33201 or 1.6, or the number of digits to the right of a decimal point in a given numeric expression. Decimal numbers are often considered to be more precise than fractions, and are favored for use in calculations in the science and engineering fields.

Fractions

Fractions are a numerical expression that expresses a ratio between a given quantity and the whole of a quantity. For example, the fraction 5/8 expresses a relationship between a whole quantity—in this case, 8, which is expressed in the example as the denominator, or the bottom term—and a partial quantity, which is 5, also known as the numerator. Fractions do not carry the same level of precision as decimal representations, but in some cases, they can present a more accurate representation than a decimal could. A prime example of this is 2/3, which is an infinite repeating number in decimal form (0.66666...) but can be succinctly presented in fractional form.

Fraction to Decimal Conversion

The basic process to convert a fraction into a decimal is to divide the numerator (or top term) by the denominator (or bottom term). For example, examine the fraction 5/8. Expressed as a long division equation, it looks like this:

$$8\overline{)5.0000}$$

In order to make this process clear, we add trailing zeros, which do not affect the value. Now, while 8 does not go into 5 as a whole number (making the first digit 0, followed by a decimal point), it will go into 50, so we solve for that, which leaves 6 with a remainder of 2. Carrying the 2 down and bringing down another 0 gives 20, which 8 goes into 2 times with a remainder of 4, which when we bring down another 0 gives 40, which 8 goes into 5 times with no remainder. Thus, 5 divided by 8, or 5/8, is equal to .625.

Decimal to Fraction Conversion

The basic process to convert a decimal expression to a fraction is to multiply the expression by whatever power of ten is necessary to make it a whole number, and write a fraction where that result is the denominator and the number of ten used to make it a whole number is the denominator. For example, examine the decimal expression 1.62. To make it a whole number, it is necessary to move the decimal point two places to the right, which requires the multiplier to be 100. So, multiplying by 100 yields 162, which will be the numerator, with the denominator being the multiplier, 100. Thus, we have 1.62 = 1.62(100)/100 = 162/100. This is accurate, but it is general practice to simplify fractions to smallest possible terms. Thus, if denominator and numerator are divided by 2, we get 162/100 ÷ (2/2) = 81/50, which further simplifies to 1 31/50.

Metrology

Variable Gages

A variable gage is an instrument used to measure a dimensional value and its deviation from a designated standard of data point, size or other dimension. Variable gages are called such because the gage itself, or a portion of it, is mutable in size or dimension, meaning it can be adjusted to a smaller or larger size depending on need. Generally, variable gages are used in situations when a piece or sub-unit of a component must be measured independent of the primary component body. Variable gages come in many forms, but despite the proliferation of modern electronic measuring devices and non-invasive measurement procedures, variable gages still tend to be mechanical devices.

Micrometers

A micrometer is a mechanical device that is generally used to measure component or sub-component thicknesses. It is also commonly used to measure slot depths and diameters, inner and outer, of slots and shafts; it is also used in measuring wire widths, as well as wire bundles. Most micrometers are hand-held devices, appearing in the form of an arc that use a screw or screws to adjust the open width, or measuring area, of the micrometer to fit snugly around the component or sub-component being measured. Micrometers are usually accurate to a few thousandths or ten-thousandths of an inch in the United States; metric versions are usually accurate to thousandths of a centimeter.

Calipers

A caliper is a mechanical device that is generally used to measure the distance between two points that are opposed, such as the size or width of an object or internal cavity. It can also be used to determine thicknesses, although it is not engineered with this application in mind. At its most basic level, a caliper is simply two metal arms joined with a single joint; the distance between the measured points is taken with the caliper arms, then compared against a ruler or other measuring device to derive the value. Calipers are not as precise as other tools, but can be used with high reliability in most production measurement situations.

Thread Wires

Thread wires are a set of wires used to calibrate tools such as thread plugs by checking thread depth. They can also be used to measure thread pitch, size and other measurements relating to shafts used for screws or bolts. Thread wires, because of their generally imprecise nature, are most often used in go/no-go measurements, meaning the point of the measurement is determine if a given part or component passes or fails, rather than falls within a range of acceptable values or can be corrected. Go/no-go measurements have a lower standard of precision and accuracy needed, so thread wires do not need to meet a higher standard that other instruments do.

Pitch Micrometers

A pitch micrometer is a device used to determine the pitch of a screw, or the distance between corresponding surfaces of two individual thread segments measured at right angles to the shaft. Pitch micrometers are very finely calibrated, and take measurements that have a high degree of precision. Because of the nature of measurements being taken, however, pitch micrometers are used in go/no-go measurements as well as in numerical measurements. Many modern pitch micrometers are a combination of traditional hand tools and electronic tools, using electrical probes and digital readouts; other than the measuring probe aspect of the tool, pitch micrometers are virtually identical to the more traditional form of the instrument.

Linear Scales

Linear scales are a general term for a measuring device that uses set intervals to derive a value. At its most basic level, linear scales can include simple measuring devices like a ruler or a yardstick, although most linear scales that quality inspectors will use in a production environment are more complex. Most linear scales that a quality inspector will work with are larger in scale and connected to an electronic device/readout for more precise measurements; some of the high-precision scales use laser pulses or magnetic probes to achieve finely differentiated measurements. Many linear scales are permanently affixed to a table or other work area, so components can be placed more accurately with regard to the scale.

Attribute Gages

An attribute gage is a device that is specifically intended to indicate if the dimension being measured fits within a predetermined tolerance or not, as well as checking both the general tolerance and functionality of a given piece. Attribute gages are most often used to determine the suitability of a small measurement or subcomponent in what are known as go/no-go measurements; while the gages derive numerical values, the measurements are generally used in a binary fashion (either they pass or do not pass). Attribute gages come in many forms, but despite the proliferation of modern electronic measuring devices and non-invasive measurement procedures, attribute gages still tend to be mechanical devices.

Snap Gages

A snap gage is a device that uses a mechanical component that moves or displaces to measure dimensions or values of a part or a portion of a part. Most snap gages are hand tools with a movable, spring-loaded piece that can be displaced easily, although some of the newer types use circuits to display readings and take more precise measurements. There are two common types: variable, which allow for adjustment by the user to take measurements, and fixed, which are factory-set to certain tolerances and are used solely for go/no-go measurement values. Variable snap gages can often be locked or adjusted to serve the same function as fixed snap gages.

Plug Gages

A plug gage is a device that generally uses two pieces of different sizes to measure hole size, depth or thread size. Plug gages come in a number of different sizes and purposes, ranging from small versions used in go/no-go measurements of components based on inner or outer diameters to large versions used to calibrate or check other instruments like micrometers. Most are roughly cylindrical in shape; the most common versions a quality inspector will see have one end used for go, or within tolerance, measurements and one end set for no-go measurements. The majority of plug gages are mechanical, but electronic and pneumatic versions are also used in some workplaces.

Thread Gages

A thread gage is a device that measures the size and accuracy of threads in a socket and/or a threading component, as well as the pitch of the thread, diameter and other dimensions. Like other attribute gages, thread gages come in a variety of types and functions, and are often used in both numerical measurements and go/no-go measurements. They are commonly cylindrical or tapered in shape. Also, like other attribute gages, they are primarily mechanical but often have electronic elements, like readouts and probes. The term thread gage generally refers to an actual instrument, but some specialized types are actually pre-measured wires, which can be wrapped around a part and thus derive a measurement using the known diameter of the wire.

Gage Blocks

A gage block is a device used to calibrate and/or set tolerances for other measuring devices. As they are used for master units, gage blocks are machined to high standards of accuracy and precision, and are generally constructed out of very durable materials, usually hardened steel, carbide or—among newer versions—ceramics. There are several basic types, including rectangular, which often come with pre-set mounting holes, wear and angle, which are notched or shaped to provide accurate representations of certain angles. Gage blocks often come with writing or marking tools so an operator or technician can easily mark the correct measurement on a component; these are often called scribing blocks.

Pin

In the context of attribute gages, a pin is a device used to measure very small distances or depths using small metal pieces. Generally, pins or pin gages are used to take go/no-go measurements only, due to their small size, although numeric measurements can be taken with pins. Pins are more accurately a sub set of plug gages, so some aspects of pins—such as various types of gage available including pneumatic and electronic—are held in common with plug gages. Most are roughly cylindrical in shape; the most common versions a quality inspector will see have one end used for go, or within tolerance, measurements and one end set for no-go measurements, although some pin gages are double-ended so when one is worn, the ends can be swapped with a minimum of downtime.

Transfer Gages

A transfer gage is a device that measures a part or distance in a two-step method; first, by taking the measurement by use of clips, arms or other separating mechanisms, and second, measuring the displacement through using an outside ruler or other measuring device. The advantage of having a tool like this is simplicity; in environments where space may be at a premium or conditions may not be conducive to immediate measurement, having a transfer gage take the measurement of the component and then being able to measure it separately can be of great convenience. Transfer gages come in many forms, but generally transfer gages still tend to be mechanical devices.

Small-Hole Gages

A small-hole gage is a device that uses two contact areas to provide a width measurement, usually two demi-spheres or, in some cases, a full sphere or irising measurement surface. As the name implies, a small-hole gage is generally a very small instrument. It is primarily used to determine diameters, although some versions also allow for depth measurements. Small-hole gages are commonly used with other types of grooves or impressions as well. Most modern small-hole gages have built-in limiting features that prevent operators for using the gage outside of its functional tolerance. Small-hole gages are, like many of the tools quality inspectors use, hand-held tools for the most part, and virtually always mechanical in nature.

Radius Gages

A radius gage is a device generally constructed of thin metal with a number of impressions and/or holes used to measure the radii of a hole or circular area. Radius gages are frequently used in a production environment to check the manufacturing equipment, specifically patterns and dies, as well as checking the finished components for quality purposes; these gages are generally used to check both internal and external radii. As a result, radius gages tend to be much simpler mechanically than other types of gages. Radius gages are, like many of the tools quality inspectors use in a production environment, hand-held tools for the most part, and virtually always mechanical in nature.

Spring Calipers

A spring caliper is a device generally consisting of a pair of arms connected by a joint that is used to obtain a displacement of length or diameter. They are often similar in appearance to the compass tool used to draw circles in many schools. As a rule, they do not have graduated measuring apparatus on them, since other measuring devices (such as a ruler or set of linear scales) are used in conjunction with spring calipers, but some models do have such built-in measuring capacities. Spring calipers are, like many of the tools quality inspectors use in a production environment, hand-held tools for the most part, and virtually always mechanical in nature.

Measurement Scales

A measurement scale is a mechanical device that is commonly used to measure a range of different values; these can range from weight to force to distance variations. For the purpose of quality measurements, scales are most often used in linear measurements. Traditional scales are either in the form of balances, where an object is weighed against known quantities, or compression scales, where an object's weight is determined from the amount of compression upon a spring. Modern scales still use these forms of weight determination, but are now more likely to use electronic circuits and different methods of sensing pressure or force, as they are more accurate and easier to read quickly.

A quality inspector can expect to use three general types of scales in the workplace. The first, and most common, is known as a dial scale, which refers to how the measurement is expressed, in this case with a rotary dial and a manual indicator that points out the value on the rotary measurement disc. A digital scale is similar to a dial scale, except that it uses a digital readout to express the value instead of a more traditional dial. Finally, the most precise type is a vernier scale, which uses two scales to express measurement values. The smaller scale is used to express minute variations of the primary measurement scale.

Electronic Gaging

Electronic gaging is the practice of using devices that utilize circuits and solenoids to take measurements rather than mechanical implements. With the increase of technology in the workplace, electronic gaging has become an increasingly common method of determining measurement values, partly due to the higher precision afforded by electronic measurements and partly due to the greater efficiency in calibrating and checking instruments. Also, many types of measurement that would have been impractical or impossible are now readily available, thanks to the influx of electronic technology. While many measuring instruments in common use in production environments are still mechanical, hand-held instruments, quality inspectors are expected to know how to use several different types of electronic gages.

Oscilloscopes

An oscilloscope is a device used to provide measurements of signal and/or voltage strength in a circuit. It expresses the wave form of a circuit—the strength of the signal—on a screen, usually a cathode ray tube (CRT) similar to most models of televisions. Oscilloscopes are commonly used in testing and quality assurance with circuits and electrical output devices, such as power supplies. The output is displayed on a graph (usually imprinted onto the screen), generally with the vertical axis representing voltage strength and the horizontal axis representing time. As a result, oscilloscopes are most frequently used to measure signals or voltages with periodic variances, i.e. cyclical in nature.

Multimeters

A multimeter is a multiple-purpose device, capable of measuring many properties of a circuit or other electrical device. Virtually all multimeters can measure a circuit's resistance, current and voltage, although many can measure other properties as well. Most common versions have a pair of leads color-coded for ground and hot wires, an analog meter for measuring strength of the property being measured, and several switches to change measurements; in quality inspections, it's necessary to keep in mind that the multimeter must be switched to the correct property before testing, as testing the wrong property can damage the multimeter, e.g. setting the multimeter to check resistance when attempting to measure voltage.

Pyrometers

A pyrometer is essentially a high-end thermometer, capable of measuring heat well in excess of normal environmental temperatures—in some cases, up to 600° Celsius. Many pyrometers can measure other types of radiation than infrared, but infrared—or heat— is the most common use of pyrometers. Pyrometers have many uses, including checking the temperatures of tires on race cars on professional circuits, but from a quality inspector standpoint, pyrometers are most commonly found in smelting or foundry environments, or in manufacturing environments where high temperatures are a part of the process. Due to the high temperatures and environmental stresses, pyrometers are virtually are electronic, and are generally non-contact instruments in nature.

Automatic Gaging

Automatic gaging is the use of electronic systems to obtain measurements without direct human intervention. Due to the increase in automation in manufacturing and testing processes, as well as an increased awareness of safety issues, automatic gaging has gained a foothold in quality inspection in recent years. Inspectors will be expected to be familiar with and use a number of varieties of automatic gaging systems, particularly in areas where automatic gaging is the only realistic approach to testing and quality assurance, such as processes that use chemical agents that are highly toxic to humans and the environment. Other examples where automatic gaging would be vital would be in environmental remediation and biological/chemical weapon disposal.

Machine Vision

Machine vision is a system that integrates computer analysis and digital photography to examine parts and mechanisms, and generates pass/fail decisions on quality. Generally, machine vision systems consist of video imaging, automated machinery or robots and computers; they can involve humans in any step, but are increasingly self-contained and capable of rendering decisions on a number of different conditions. Machine vision is intended to act as both a testing platform and a guidance system for automated manufacturing systems. There are several reasons for machine vision implementations, including efficiency, safety (for manufacturing environments where having human observers may present a risk to the observers) and greater conformity in the final product.

Ultrasonic

Ultrasonic is, in the context of quality inspection, a non-destructive testing system that uses sound waves pitched beyond human hearing ranges (generally about 20 kHz – 2 MHz, with some variation) to examine parts for flaws and parameter matching. The principle is the same as sonar, which uses sound waves and the reflection off surfaces and objects to display a map, and is very similar to the ultrasound machines used in doctors' offices for pre-natal checkups.

Differences in product density and structure will reflect sound waves back differently, as will empty spaces, and the information can be used to develop a picture of potential flaws and trouble areas in a component.

X-Rays

X-ray is, in the context of quality inspection, a non-destructive testing system that uses short-wavelength (generally between 0.1 and 100 angstroms), high-energy beams to examine internal structures for flaws and parameter matching. Essentially the same as in medical x-ray systems, an x-ray testing system beams radiation through a component. Differences in product density and structure will block the radiation differently, as will empty spaces, and the information can be used to develop a picture of potential flaws and trouble areas in a component, or verify that the component meets specification. Some materials block x-ray radiation more efficiently than others, so with some types of material such as lead, x-ray may be a less effective testing system.

Lasers

Laser is, in the context of quality inspection, a measurement system that uses beams of highly focused coherent light (meaning all one frequency) to obtain measurement values to several magnitudes of precision. Structurally, a laser is essentially an empty space bracketed by mirrors with a gas or other lasing material in the space that light is pumped into, stimulated and reflected into a beam of amplified, monochromatic light which is then sent through an aperture. As the wavelength is carefully controlled as part of the process, and the beam is by necessity tightly focused, lasers are capable of numerous uses, including measurement of distances to an extremely high degree of accuracy and precision.

Pneumatic Gaging

Pneumatic gages are measuring devices that use air pressure to derive measurement values for pressure, cross-sections and wind profiles, among other values. There are several types of pneumatic gaging widely used in quality inspections, primarily because pneumatic gages are very quick and accurate, particularly in high-volume production workplaces, where it is likely such instruments can make use of an existing pneumatic system. Pneumatic gages can be hand-held units, but they are often larger, stationary machines due to the volume and power of the pneumatic system; these devices are generally very complex units. Because pressure is an integral part of pneumatic gaging systems, the indicators are generally analog meters, which provide a clearer picture than digital readouts might in similar situations.

Air Columns

An air column is a device that uses an enclosed column of air to measure pressure differentials. They can be used for a number of measurement types, including air pressure—as in an barometer, for example, which is used in meteorology and pressure testing of components in many industries—and resonance checking. At their simplest, such devices are really hollow, enclosed columns that can be pressurized or emptied of air in order to take measurements or perform experiments. Sonic testing is often performed with air columns, as they can be easily manipulated to produce tones of varying frequency and sound; the study of how waves move through material is also a frequent use of air columns.

Probes

Within the context of pneumatic gaging, a probe is a device that uses a small mobile measurement component to measure pressure flows and differentials. They are most often used to check hole and slot measurements against previously determined specifications for go/no-go decisions, though they have a number of different uses. Depending on the use of the instrument and the components being measured, the level of precision a probe is capable of rendering can vary, but in general, probes are used to measure distances within very narrow tolerances. As with most modern gaging instruments, electronic versions are quickly becoming more common, due to their greater precision and accuracy when compared to their mechanical counterparts.

Rings

Within the context of pneumatic gaging, a ring is a device that uses a circular component to measure pressure tolerances at low and high ends of a given pressure range. They are also, and more commonly in a production or quality assurance environment, used to measure specified dimensions of pins, shafts, threaded cylinders and other cylindrical objects against tolerances and are often used, like probes, in conjunction with other gages. Rings themselves are mechanical in nature, but they are often used in concert with electronic devices and readouts. Unless working with outsized components or in environments not amenable to human observers, rings are virtually always tools of the hand-held variety.

Selecting Gages

The first factor is the feature or characteristic to be measured; does the gage measure that particular value to be obtained? Another factor to consider is the applicable tolerance. The gage must measure the feature to within the acceptable tolerance as dictated by the product or part's needs, not the gage's. Accuracy resolution is the third factor to be considered. Can a measurement be made to a level of accuracy needed for quality inspection and/or manufacturing? Also, the capability of the instrument needs to be considered; if it is not sufficiently versatile or usable in a quality inspection situation, it cannot be used. Finally, the type of measurement the gage can make must be considered. There are different types of measurement a quality inspector can perform, and some will not be applicable in certain situations.

10:1 Rule

The 10:1 rule states that a master part or calibration piece should have a tolerance that is 10% of the tolerance of the part being measured, or in other words, that the tolerance of the master is one-tenth of the part. This rule is not a fixed regulation, but it is a practical rule of thumb, in that only in certain situations will a tolerance smaller than the 10:1 rule dictates be needed. The 10:1 rule is generally used in go/no-go measurements, meaning the part is being measured on a pass (go)/fail (no-go) basis. Generally, the 10:1 rule is only used in hand tool measurements, as automatic gaging is generally a few magnitudes more accurate in measuring.

Measurement Types

A quality inspector can expect to perform three types of measurements on the job. The first and most common measurement type is direct measurement, where an absolute value for a value is determined, e.g. diameter or weight. The second type of measurement is differential, where a value is taken relative to a baseline value. Differential measurements are most often taken in situations of varying strength or change marked over time, such as voltage levels or stress fractures. The third type of measurement is transfer, where a value is measured after a transaction of some type to determine the aftereffects of the transaction, such as power or heat transfer.

Cleaning Gages

Several factors must be considered when cleaning the various gages used in quality inspection. Is the gage being cleaned as part of normal maintenance, or is there contamination on it from use? Depending on the substances used (strain gages, for example, are most often used with putty or other sealing agents), water or isopropyl alcohol may be sufficient; some substances may require solvents. Is the gage constructed of material that will be damaged or warped by normal cleaning methods? Fine-resolution gages may need different cleaning tools or methods than hand tools, which can be cleaned by hand with cloths or brushes. Automatic gages may have built-in cleaning procedures, which the quality inspector should be aware of before use. Also, inspectors should be up to date on any applicable SDS for the cleaning products before using, including their location in case of a spill.

Handling Gages

When handling gages, quality inspectors must keep in mind several factors. First, the nature of the gage's intended use must be considered. Is the gage sufficiently precise and sufficiently constructed for its intended use? Depending on where and how it's used, the tool could be too precise or too fragile to use if this aspect is ignored. Will the physical environment affect the gage? Humidity and temperature can affect measurements of the gage. Is it being used in the intended fashion? Hand tools are generally built to different scales and standards of durability, and the inspector must also consider this. Also, will the gage being used affect the part to be measured? Some gages may damage the surface or operating environment of the part if used incorrectly.

Storing Gages

Proper storage of gages requires quality inspectors to consider several factors. First, the storage area must be clean and free of contamination, as this could affect the accuracy and precision of the gages, as well as damage the gages. Additionally, the storage area must be dry, as water can damage gages over long periods of exposure. To minimize environmental effects, the storage area should have a controlled climate, with temperature and humidity being the primary factors to watch for; metal expansion and contraction can decalibrate the gages and make measurements unreliable. Finally, the storage area should be clearly marked and easily accessible to inspectors.

Gage Correlation

There are different ways to perform gage correlation, or the aligning of gages so that a measurement taken with one gage will yield a similar result with the other gage(s), depending on the intent of the correlation. Using a lab standard or master to synchronize gages is one way to perform gage correlation. Another way is to manually synchronize one gage with another, which is similar to using a lab standard, except manual synchronization only aligns one gage at a time. Using a manual-to-automated process—for example, manually inputting measurement values into a program and allowing the software to use the values to synchronize the gages—is another method, and an increasingly popular method of correlation.

Surface Plates

A surface plate is a flat table, generally machined to be level to a high degree of accuracy, which is used as a reference plane for various measurements. Usually made from stone, steel or other material that displays low degrees of fluctuation based on environmental conditions, the surface plate is required to be precisely machined, as it is used as a baseline for measurement, marking, layout and preparing for tooling. The table can be any size, but must be sufficiently large to support the necessary tools for measuring and qualifying parts, as well as the parts themselves. Surface plates are the basis for confidence in many measurements.

There are several types of equipment commonly found used with surface plates. The first device type is height gages, devices used to measure vertical dimension of various parts and components. Height gages are also used to create repeated markings on vertical surfaces. Another type of equipment is V-blocks, which are commonly used to measure and mark cylindrical components.

Indicators, or devices used to detect the presence of other components or conditions, are another type of commonly used surface plate equipment. Indicators are most often used with electrical measuring devices, although they are frequently used with chemical agents as well.

Angle Measurement Instruments

Quality inspectors will frequently use three common types of angle measurement instruments. Protractors are generally used to measure angles or create arcs; they can be semicircular in shape or consist of two arms connected by a joint. Sine bars are also used to measure angles; they generally consist of a single bar connected to two cylinders with a known metrical relationship to the main bar, which is the reference sample. The main bar becomes the hypotenuse of a right triangle, allowing measurement of the other angles to be taken. Angle blocks are simply blocks generally shaped as a right triangle, which can be fitted into other angles for measurement.

Specialized Inspection Equipment

Quality inspectors frequently refer to specialized inspection equipment to measure weight and mass. The term weights refers to standardized blocks of materials whose weight has been determined to a certain level of precision; these blocks are used in conjunction with a balance, a type of scale that compares an item of unknown weight to a collection of weights chosen by the measurer in order to determine weight (or mass, since the relationship between mass and weight in a uniform gravitational field is well-defined). A scale is a more general type of measuring device to determine weight and/or mass; scales can include balances or spring-driven devices, among others, that use compression to measure force due to gravity, and thus derive a value for weight.

Measuring Equipment

In order to measure **finish**, quality inspectors often turn to a trio of instrument types. The first type is a profilometer, which is most commonly used to derive a value for the surface roughness of an object, as defined by a relative measurement of the difference between the peaks and valleys of a surface. A profile tracer, another commonly used type of instrument, uses a probe connected to a rotating drum to create a topological map of a surface, enabling a highly accurate picture of a surface to be created. Finally, a fingernail comparator is an instrument that provides a rough but very quick approximate value for surface finish; it is generally used in situations where an approximate value is of more value than a more accurate value would be.

There are three general types of equipment quality inspectors use when measuring **shape and profile** of a given component. A comparator is a high-precision instrument, usually electronic, that compares a component to a standardized shape/profile and provides measurements for deviances from the standard; comparators are also used to measure voltages or currents. Roundness testers are high-precision instruments that generally combine high-accuracy probes and software to measure arc, off-centeredness, thickness and a number of other values to determine within a given level of precision the circularity of a component. Precision spindles are simply slender rods machined to very high precision which are used with bearings to maintain very high tolerances of rotary spin or measuring small distances.

Optical Equipment

Quality inspectors frequently refer to specialized optical equipment to perform inspections. Optical comparators are instruments that display large images of components, usually on a projector screen or blank wall, so that inspectors can examine the component features easily. Optical flats are highly machined plates of material, usually transparent materials like glass, that are specifically engineered to have minimal surface imperfections; these are used as masters for other plates that are used to measure surface roughness and/or imperfections. Microscopes are simply arrangements of lenses used to view features and objects to small to be seen by the naked eye; they are generally used by inspectors to magnify or view features of components. Reference specimens are simply components that are used as a baseline in measurements, particularly when destructive testing is being performed.

Digital Vision Systems

Digital vision systems, or equipment that uses computers and digitization to create highly accurate pictures of components, are increasingly used by quality inspectors to refine optical inspections. Digital cameras are a major part of this; similar to consumer models commonly used, these cameras use sensors and microchips, rather than lenses and film, to capture pictures and store them in electronic format. Online surface inspection is a high-precision variant of a digital vision system, using arrays of high-performance cameras, software and imaging systems (some with viewing capabilities in the microscopic range) to examine the surface of components and/or materials for defects and conformance to tolerances. Other forms of digital vision systems use false-color processing (for measurements taken in non-visible spectrums) to display attributes not visible in regular light, and/or different tools, such as scanning electron microscopes or ultrasound viewers, to examine components and surfaces.

Coordinate Measuring Machines

A coordinate measuring machine is a large instrument, generally consisting of a table with a bridge structure on top that moves down the length of the table and contains two stylus or probe instruments that can move along two other axes, thus providing for three axes of measurement. One of the primary issues in using a CMM is in locating functional datums with which to measure the component, as these datums are dependent on how the part is made, the function of the part and how the part will be inspected. Defining functional datums can change relative to how the part or component is measured; also, the use of orthogonal (i.e. at right angles) or non-orthogonal datums must also be weighed. These factors will also define the target points (where datums will be measured) and target areas (areas where the three axes for measurement will meet).

Calibration

Calibration, or the process of adjusting and correcting an instrument so that its measurements conform to a standard of relevance in providing values, is one of the most necessary parts of quality inspection. It is intended to provide a standard of reliability for measurements and instrument usage, as well as provide a baseline for other instrumentation. Calibration is also necessary for performance and usage of a component or system, particularly for units that work at very high levels of precision and/or accuracy, because components that are not calibrated may fail before their projected date, as components that work outside a narrow range may be subject to destructive failure in some instances.

Calibration Intervals

Establishing calibration intervals is necessary in order to properly use instruments; the intervals may be based on manufacturer recommendations, but will primarily depend on the application and values needed from the instruments. Once the necessary intervals are decided upon, then calibration can be performed (often by a professional lab or service provider). Afterward, interval monitoring can be performed on a regular basis as part of instrument maintenance, either through regular testing of the instrument (particularly for electronic instruments) or comparison against a standard or master version. Monitoring also calls for repeated testing/comparison, against different components or materials and, if applicable, in different environmental conditions the instrument might be used in.

Calibration Records

Maintaining records of calibration are vital for a number of reasons. First, accurate records are necessary for passing audits and maintaining ISO certification. Also, having records allows a chain of events to be reconstructed in case of instrument failure or defect, so that the cause can be located and remedied. If an environmental or usage condition is causing premature equipment failure or product issues, records can help address that as well. Having documented procedures for calibration are also important for continuity of knowledge and lack of downtime, if a calibration provider becomes unavailable and/or the instrument owner needs to switch providers. Finally, having accurate records can assist in training of technicians or other instrument professionals.

Coding Schemes

Coding schemes, or structured methods of organizing information so it can be interpreted by other users and/or instruments, are a necessary part of calibration and instrument usage, as unstructured data is virtually useless in a production or research environment. In order to utilize data in calibration procedures, it must be expressed in a fashion the calibrating technician and/or machine can interpret, which means it must be coded correctly. By the same token, data that is taken in measurement format and then utilized by the instrument(s) must also be coded correctly (for example, data that will be displayed on a screen needs to be coded as video data) in order to be read or output correctly.

Calibration Standards

There are two different standards organizations that quality inspectors may need to refer to when calibrating instruments. At the national level and for working standards, the US National Institute of Standards and Technology (NIST) sets the benchmarks for calibration standards. However, when working with international standards and/or settling disputes with SI units, the International Bureau of Weights and Measures—which is charged under the Meter Convention of 1875 and by diplomatic treaty other signatory nations with maintaining the official standards for SI units—is the final authority. NIST is a partner in setting international standards, but is responsible for making determinations for English units still used in the United States.

Traceability

Traceability, or the interrelation of the information in each step of a process chain to a measurement standard, is vital in calibration and maintenance of measuring instruments because when traceability is maintained, it maintains a high level of reliability for measurements, establishes a threshold for accuracy and assists in maintaining an unbroken chain of record. Also, when traceability maintains a defined relationship between measurements and a pre-defined standard, the level of uncertainty, or variance in a given measurement, can be rigorously defined and maintained. Since maintaining a record chain is important in maintaining audit verifiability and ISO certification, traceability is valuable in a bureaucratic sense as well as a purely functional fashion.

Environmental Concerns

Temperature can have a number of effects on gage calibration, depending on the method of measurement and the material/component being measured. Materials can expand or contract, depending on the differential change, and change the intervals measured or alter the data derived from measuring. Pressure of certain gases may rise or fall depending on the change in molecular motion, throwing off measurements or decalibrating instruments. Also, properties such as electrical conductivity can be altered by temperature, thus affecting measurements of voltage or current. Unless measuring for properties in extreme environmental conditions or to determine how the component will perform under specific conditions, most measurements should generally be taken in a baseline environment.

Humidity can also have a number of effects on gage calibration, depending on the method of measurement and the material/component being measured. Changes in moisture in the air can change the electrical conductivity of components (e.g. dry conditions increase conductivity, moist ones inhibit it), leading to changes in the measurement or, in extreme cases, the component itself. Moisture can also have a corrosive effect on some materials, causing premature component fatigue and altering measurements, as well as affecting rigidity and, in turn, shape/profile measurements. Unless measuring for properties in extreme environmental conditions or to determine how the component will perform under specific conditions, most measurements should generally be taken in a baseline environment.

Vibration also effects measuring instrument. Highly sensitive instruments can be physically knocked out of calibration by excessive movement or by the transfer of energy as vibration; with certain electronic instruments, the reporting capacity can also be affected. Excessive amounts of vibration can also have a negative effect on the structural integrity of an instrument, particularly the most delicate parts and/or circuits of an instrument. As vibration can manifest as sound, it is also possible that vibration could mask auditory cues an inspector could use to make other determinations. Unless measuring for properties in extreme environmental conditions or to determine how the component will perform under specific conditions, most measurements should generally be taken in a baseline environment.

Cleanliness can have a number of potential effects on a measuring instrument. Depending on the precision and sensitivity of the instrument, even a small amount of contamination can throw the instrument out of calibration and create incorrect measurements. This is especially an issue with high-caliber precise instruments, but is present with all measuring instruments. Also, because of the delicacy and extremely low error tolerance of some parts and tools, any contamination can cause physical damage to the component, and possibly to the manufacturing process, as well as introduce the possibility of corrosive elements to the component. Unless measuring for properties in extreme environmental conditions or to determine how the component will perform under specific conditions, most measurements should generally be taken in a baseline environment.

Out-of-Calibration Instruments

Having out-of-calibration instruments can have a multitude of effects. First, depending on the sensitivity of the instruments and the components being measured, it can have a negative physical effect on the instruments and the components, whether through misalignment, contamination or some other factor. Furthermore, if the miscalibration is not immediately apparent, products being inspected may have measurements that are out of tolerance, which has a negative impact both on the functional lifetime of the component but the warranties or other agreements that may apply to the component. This can lead to component and product failures, as well as costly repair and replacement issues, as well as damage to the business relationship between the manufacturer and the consumer.

Resolving Calibration Issues

Out-of-calibration issues need to be addressed right away, particularly in a production environment. The first thing that should be done would be ensuring the instruments are actually out of calibration; this could be done by checking the instruments against test quantities to discover how far out of calibration they are. Once tested, the next step would be to discontinue working with the OOC instruments. Replacing the instruments temporarily with calibrated substitutes would be a good option, if calibration services are not immediately available. Re-calibrating the instruments against a known good master or, in some cases, an accurately calibrated instrument is another possible action. For most instruments, the best option would be to contact the lab or service provider responsible for tool calibration and make arrangements to re-calibrate the instruments.

Measurement System Analysis

Measurement system analysis is the examination of a given system of measurement for the purpose of determining the level of precision in any particular value derived from that system. Performing a full system analysis is done to qualify a system and ensure that the system meets all expectations in precision, as well as accuracy and stability. There are several factors that must be determined before performing an analysis; many of these factors are or should be known before a system is put to use, as they will be part of the system's overall specifications. Measurement system analysis should always be carried out prior to any measurements or decision-making based on derived values.

Bias

Determining bias, or the difference between the average of measurements of a given part or component and the actual measurement of that same part, is critical to establishing the accuracy of a measurement system. In order to properly identify the bias, it is necessary to conduct a series of calibration measurements, making sure that the entire range of permissible (or possible) process values is covered in the samples. The actual calculation of bias is simply done by taking the arithmetic mean of the sample measurement values (referred to as x-bar) and subtracting the reference value; the difference is the bias of the system. If the value for the bias or the bias percentage (derived by dividing the bias by the process variation, or the value of six standard deviations) is excessively high, then the measurement system needs to be adjusted, as the systemic inaccuracy is outside of acceptable bounds.

Stability

Stability is another vital aspect of a measurement system; it refers to consistency of measurement of the same sample set over time. Stability is related to the reliability of a system more than accuracy or precision, as it is possible for a system to be inaccurate and imprecise, yet be extremely stable. Another way to view stability would be the absence of variation other than random fluctuations. Stability is derived by taking multiple measurements of a reference sample over a pre-set period of time and comparing them to ensure that the sample measurements are falling within an acceptable range. Stability is vital to determine, since it is a major criteria for repeated and continuous usage of a system.

Accuracy

Accuracy is yet another vital aspect of a measurement system, and in the short-term, probably the most important. Accuracy is defined as the level of agreement between a component's measured value and its actual value, or more simply, the quality of the measurement of a component. When performing a calibration of a tool or instrument, accuracy is one of the primary goals of the calibration; the other goal is precision, or the closeness of randomly selected measurements relative to the master value, generally taken from a reference sample. A system that does not meet accuracy standards is unsuitable for use in a production environment, so determining and/or correcting the accuracy of a measurement system is paramount.

Linearity

Linearity is another property that affects the use of a measurement system over time; it refers to the persistence of bias over a range of measurements carried out by the measurement system. In other words, a system possesses good linearity if a measurement of a component at the smallest end of the measurement scale displays the same degree of bias as a measurement taken near the middle of the scale and a measurement taken at the higher end of the scale. The linearity measure of a given system is a major factor in determining the reliability of that system, as well as determining where potential issues may lie in the system or its instrumentation.

Repeatability and Reproducibility

Repeatability and reproducibility studies, or R&R studies, are an important part of the checks and balance system quality inspectors must use with a measurement system. Repeatability refers to the property of a system to yield the same measurements of the same part when being measured by an operator at different times. Reproducibility refers to the property of multiple operators obtaining the same set of measurements using identical instruments at different times; while it tends to be geared more toward operators than equipment, it is still a vital part of ensuring a measurement system meets qualifications. The point of R&R studies is to ensure that a system is sufficiently accurate and precise to meet the R&R standards required by a production system.

Inspection & Test

Geometric Dimensioning and Tolerancing

Geometric dimensioning and tolerancing, or GDT, is a structured methodology for deriving precise definitions for the geometrical profiles and dimensional values for mechanical components in a system. In its implementation in quality inspection and engineering, GDT is a graphical language used in blueprints and specifications to define the shape and dimensions of the parts being described; the historical ability of industry to quickly ramp up production and manufacture mass quantities of products is due in part to developing GDT and its widespread acceptance. GDT is the de facto standard for mechanical drafting, both hand-drawn and computer-assisted, and has been used in multiple industries, including aerospace and industrial design, for several decades now.

Blueprints

Blueprints are the technical layouts of an architecture or component, drawn out to scale, often using GDT symbols. Depending on the level of complexity of the architecture or component being depicted, blueprints can be relatively simple or tremendously complicated. For example, blueprints of a building may include floor plans, layouts for electrical, plumbing and HVAC systems, elevations, wall plans, site plans, details about the construction and materials, and so forth. Most quality inspectors will likely work with documents of a smaller degree of complexity, but it is vital to understand what blueprints depict in order to perform structural analyses and make intelligent decisions, particularly when making engineering or construction decisions.

Technical Drawing Title

The title of a technical drawing is more than simply the name of the drawing itself; standard practice dictates that the title concisely explain the type of drawing it is—whether it be a detailed document, general view or specific subtype of drawing—and what the drawing represents. The title is always placed within a title block, which is generally in the form of a border along at least one side of the drawing area; the title block can actually be viewed as the entire form, of which the drawing itself is only a subsection. The title block contains all the information needed to classify, identify, read and interpret, and eventually archive the drawing, making it a vital part of the drawing.

Tolerance

Tolerance, in the context of blueprints or technical drawings, means the amount of leeway in a given measurement value to allow for imperfections, environmental factors or other conditions that could cause a part or component to fall outside the stated measurements needed. The value recorded for tolerance on a technical drawing is the maximum allowable value that a given measurement value can be off from the stated value in the drawing or plan; any component that falls outside the stated tolerance must fail quality inspection. As a result, the tolerance measurement is a vital one to know and understand, and its inclusion in blueprints and technical drawings is a necessity.

Revision Blocks

A revision block is a section on a blueprint or technical drawing that maintains a list of all revisions that have been made to the drawing, along with the reviser's name or initials and listing the changes made. In some cases, the revision block may also have reasons for the changes being made. Having a revision block is vital for technical drawings, because it allows for accounting of change and provides a paper trail, which is invaluable for future revisions and audits. Revision blocks also allow for returning to an earlier version if a suggested change turns out to be infeasible for engineering or manufacturing reasons, as well as provide a historical model for the component or part.

Notes

Not everything can be accurately conveyed on a blueprint or technical drawing, even with a rich graphical language like GDT; this is where notes, or written information that covers details that cannot be communicated through GDT or draftwork, come in. Notes are usually used to provide additional information for special objects or features, and are recorded in upper-case letters in order to achieve maximum legibility if the drawing or plan is altered in size or photocopied repeatedly. They may be connected to leading symbols, such as arrows, that refer to the specific subject of the notes if it is not immediately clear from the notes what the subject is.

Scale

Scale is the ratio of the dimensions depicted on a technical drawing or blueprint to the actual dimensions of the object in the real world. For example, if a part is drawn to have a length of two inches on a blueprint, and the part is actually ten feet in length when constructed, then the scale of the drawing is 1:60, as two inches multiplied by 60 is equal to 120 inches, which is ten feet. Scale must be strictly defined and adhered to when drafting plans or drawings, as failure to do so will result in manufacturing error, since the measurements will be significantly off when the drawings are consulted during the build process.

Drawing Views

Drawing views are specific formats for viewing a component or part in a technical viewing; more accurately, drawing views are the viewpoint from which the drawing or plan is made. There are several standard types of drawing views commonly used, ranging from the pictorial view, which is generally a three-dimensional rendering with the component tilted at an angle to show its depth, to the orthogonal view, which is a two dimensional view taken from a viewpoint perpendicular to the part; orthogonal views frequently come in multiple versions, in order to capture all sides of the component. Other views include exploded, where the components or parts are displayed in the order they would be installed in but physically separated in order to show their relationship, and cross section, which removes half of the component in order to show the internal structure.

Technical Details

Technical details are the notations and figures that fill in the smaller, sometimes less strictly defined data points that go into creating a technical drawing or plan. The overall structure of a room or building—floor plan, number of walls, stairwells, rooms and windows—is part of the general drawing, but things like the numerical values of measurements and the specific type of lighting would be considered technical details. These are generally laid out based on a pair of primary sources: the product specifications, or the required measurements and construction for the various components, and the control documents, which define what materials and ancillary products are acceptable for use on a given project.

ASME Y14.5M Standard

The Y14.5M Standard is a set of definitions and guidelines set out by the American Society of Mechanical Engineers (ASME) to codify and standardize the set of symbols and rules that make up the language of geometric dimensioning and tolerancing, or GDT. The ASME released the latest version of this standard, which defines the common language for GDT across industries and nations, in 1994, intending for GDT to more fully live up to its stated purpose of describing the purpose or intent of a component or assembly from the standpoint of ensuring accuracy in representing the stated geometries. Note that the ASME standard is only applied to drawings and blueprints done in the US; other countries may follow the standard, but ASME has no jurisdiction to enforce it.

Position Tolerance

Position tolerance is a specific subset of tolerances that quality inspectors work with regularly. It refers to a zone or area within which a part or component's center axis of center plane is allowed to be off the theoretically true value. For example, if a component has a post that is inserted into a hole designed to hold that post in position, the post may have a position tolerance of 0.001 mm, meaning it can be 0.001 mm offset and still fall within acceptable values. Older blueprints or technical drawings may refer to true position tolerance, which is the older term for position tolerance. Position tolerance is represented by a symbol that looks like crosshairs with the center point set inside a circle.

Bonus Tolerance

Bonus tolerance is a condition where excess tolerance that is not being used in one dimension can be applied to another dimension, if related. In order for bonus tolerance to be used, the tolerance levels have to be defined as being at least material condition (LMC) or maximum material condition (MMC) in order for bonus tolerances to be computed; if the tolerance levels are labeled as regardless of feature size (RFS), no bonus tolerance is allowable. Bonus tolerances are most often computed when a part is fit into another and tolerances for size and position need to be computed; since size affects position and vice versa, this is a prime example of how bonus tolerance can come into play.

Part Alignment and Datum Structure

When describing a part or component, the datum structure—or a set of defined points on the part or component that are accompanied by data that delineates the spatial relationship between the defined points such that the representation can be scaled easily regardless of actual size—is by necessity defined first. Since the datum structure lays out the spatial organization of the component, part alignment, or the arrangement of sub-parts or components, is by definition a subset of the datum structure. Therefore, by defining the datum structure, part alignment follows naturally as a consequence. Conversely, by working backwards, a component with a defined part alignment can, at least in part, be used to derive a datum structure.

Acceptable Quality Level

Acceptable quality level, or acceptance quality level as it is commonly referred to, is the lowest product average of a series of components or products that is allowed in the production of said components for use in a production environment or for transaction. Often measured as a percentage or ratio, it is measured against a set number of pieces and not against individual parts, as individual parts represent too small a sample size to make statistically adequate judgments as a whole. In order to create a valid acceptance quality level for a production environment, a rules scheme with exceptions, allowances for discontinuation and strictly defined criteria must be created and enforced.

Random Sampling

Random sampling is the process where members of a lot or collection of items to be tested are selected using a repetitious process designed to give every individual member of the collection an equal and non-dependent probability of being selected in the sampling. Using random sampling is considered the best way to perform certain kinds of quality inspection, as it reduces the possibility of skewing the quality results by favoring one sub-batch of products for factors perceived to have an effect on the overall rankings. Random sampling can be done by a number of methods, including blind selection of samples, but should be done consistently once a method has been chosen.

Value of Lot Size

Lot size, or the number of products or components in a lot or collection, is necessary to know because it will determine the values of quality inspection values. Both acceptable quality level and random sampling sizes will be determined by lot size, since both are expressed as ratios; although a value can be defined for both, the absolute value cannot be known until the lot size has been decided. For example, if the acceptable quality level is 2%, then for a lot of 100 components, that would mean that a maximum of 2 can fail to meet quality standards; however, if the lot is 500, then 10 components is the maximum allowable of fail-to-meet components.

Acceptance Number

Acceptance number is similar to acceptance quality level; it is the largest number of items found in a given lot that do not meet quality standards but allows the lot in total to meet quality standards. Acceptance numbers are for individual lots or components, not an entire run or process, but the acceptance number is generally the same for individual lots as the acceptance quality level for an entire run. This similarity, however, is not a required rule; the quality level for an entire run, for example, may be slightly higher than would be achieved if every lot met the acceptance number. As with acceptance quality levels, in order to create a valid acceptance number for a production environment, a rules scheme with exceptions, allowances for discontinuation and strictly defined criteria must be created and enforced.

Sampling Plans

As the name implies, a sampling plan is a process document that outlines the acceptable size of a sample for a given lot in a production process and the attributes or criteria that make the sample acceptable or unacceptable. The sampling plan does not, however, define how the sample is to be selected; it only covers the sample itself and how it is to be defined for purposes of quality inspection. This plan should be part of a rules scheme with exceptions, allowances for discontinuation and strictly defined criteria that must be created and enforced in order to create a valid sample for use in quality inspection purposes in a production environment.

Inspection Types

Inspection, or the process of examining parts or components for conformance to quality standards using judgment, measurement and/or testing where appropriate, is a process that has many variations, depending on the immediate goal. Normal inspection, for example, is what is performed when the quality level is expected to meet norms, i.e. nothing out of the ordinary. An inspection may be tightened or loosened if the process is not catching enough errors or is needlessly rigorous; in some cases, particularly after a major change or accident, a 100 percent inspection may be performed, meaning every attribute and measurement is examined (this is a very thorough process, but very time-consuming). If the presence or absence of a certain attribute needs to be captured, an inspection by attributes may be carried out.

Timeliness

Timeliness is a measure of the value of a particular measurement relative to the chronological space in which the measurement occurs, specifically the interval between the measurement and the reporting of the resultant value. When a measurement is referred to as being timely, it means the interval between the measuring and the report was small enough to fall within tolerance intervals, and is of use. Timeliness is usually used when taking measurements of attributes or conditions that change over time, as opposed to physical measurements of components that do not appreciably change size or other factors. Examples of this would include volume, current flow and pressure, all of which can be considered variable based on physical conditions.

Inspection Planning

Inspection planning, or the creation of a structure and timeframe for conducting inspections of a workspace or production area, is vital in creating and enforcing a framework for quality evaluation and feedback. The planning process involves not just detailing the items and procedures for inspection, but the timelines, qualified personnel, recordkeeping and feedback mechanisms. When completed correctly, the planning process lays out a beginning-to-end document that details what will be inspected, who will do it, what they'll be looking for, how to record what they find and how to fix it, which can be as complicated process as creating the original component(s). This document can be used for training, audit purposes and refinement of production processes.

Incoming Material Inspection

Incoming material inspection, or the evaluation of materials or components before being utilized in the production process, is often utilized to ensure the pre-production materials are up to production standards and can be used safely and efficiently. It is generally the first inspection carried out, though not all production environments use this process. Depending on the processes involved, incoming material inspection can check for a variety of different attributes, but the goals and qualifications for incoming material inspection, among other inspection types if applicable, should be laid out in the inspection planning stage, as well as alternate procedures (levels of acceptability, possible procedures to raise quality to acceptable standards) and record-keeping practices.

First Article Inspection

First article inspection, or the evaluation of the first component or product created in a production run, is generally used as a benchmark for the production process. Rather than make quality judgments, first article inspections are used to evaluate the process itself: conformance with expected results, deviation from tolerance levels, and evaluation of potential flaws in the process are all part of the first article inspection process. First article inspection is considered part of the calibration process more than a quality inspection, since the feedback is often immediate and may not necessarily involve quality inspectors, and it may be repeated several times depending on the results and the deviance from the expected results.

In-Process Inspection

In-process inspection is one of the most valuable types of quality inspection available, because it allows for fine-tuning the production process through real-time data as well as quickly identifying materials that do not meet quality standards. Making the inspection process part of the production methodology also allows flaws in the process to be identified, such as bottlenecks in the process flow or opportunities for increased training, as well as places where the process can be redesigned for greater efficiency. However, in-process inspection can also be the most difficult to perform, because it does require a heavier design and engineering emphasis when designing the process, as well as increased attention and complexity in the production process itself.

Final Inspection

Final inspection, or the evaluation of a completed part or component to ensure the completed object meets specifications satisfactorily, is used as an evaluative tool for both the result of the production process and the process itself. Though not as specific a tool as in-process inspection for identifying flawed sub-processes, final inspection can create a holistic conceptualization of the entire process that can be used to further perfect a production set of procedures or affirm that the process works as designed. Of all the quality inspection types, final inspection is the type that is most nearly universal; there is virtually no production process presently in force does not utilize a final inspection process.

Order of Application

The concept of order of application—essentially the order in which a series of steps are taken—is necessary to consider when setting up an inspection cycle, because each type performed will have an effect on the process as a whole and on the next type to be performed. With regard to inspections, the general order is as followed: Incoming material inspections are to be done first, as concerns about materials need to be addressed before looking at process. Next to be done would be in-process, which can be considered part of production, which leads to first article inspection. In-process and first article inspections can be thought of as a loop within the production process, since first article is done as a calibration and may be repeated a few times. Finally, after the loop is completed and the process is underway, final inspections will be performed on completed products.

Bias

Bias is a property that is present in virtually all measurement systems, and must be accounted for when recording values. Bias is simply the extent to which a given set of measurements of an attribute are off from the true measurement of that attribute, either too high or too low. The value for the bias is derived from the mean of the given set, so bias cannot be determined from an individual measurement; generally, it is accepted that it takes three measurements to determine a value for the bias. Bias can also refer to a flaw in the analysis of the measurement data or to presuppositions by the quality inspector that skew observations, but in a quality inspection context, bias almost always refers to the measurement system and not to any subsequent data modeling.

Fatigue

Fatigue is the failure of material or mechanical properties due to repetitive stresses applied to a component over a period of time. As a result of material fatigue, measurements can have a value different than their true value, and cause an incorrect assessment of a component's fitness to function. The most common sign of fatigue in materials is cracking, although deformation can result as well; inability to retain a set configuration is a common side effect of material fatigue. Due to the repetitive nature of stresses over periods of time, fatigue can cause a component to fail, sometimes catastrophically, even if stresses far below the component's normal acceptable range are applied. Fatigue can also refer to the physical condition of being tired, a state quality inspectors want to avoid as much as possible, as physical fatigue leads to impaired perception and judgment, which leads to incorrect measurements and quality decisions.

Flinching

Flinching is the condition where a quality inspector notices a borderline defect (i.e. something that is extremely close to passing acceptable quality level) during an inspection and fails to note it as a defect. The reasons for flinching are numerous; they can range from poor perception and misjudgment of severity to unwillingness to prevent a component from continuing (either through being in a hurry or unwilling to continue the task). However, flinching is in itself something to avoid, as even borderline defects can cause catastrophic failure in later inspection tests or even in an operational environment. One of the entire reasons to have a quality inspection is to be thorough in accumulating data, and flinching runs directly counter to that.

Product Traceability

Product traceability, or the ability to follow a chain of events and construct the history, location and status of a product using recorded information about the product, is a valuable trait to have for quality inspections. Being able to trace the history of a product or component allows the inspector to check the history against known processes, track changes or modifications to a product, and find potential causes of any issue that a quality inspection might uncover. Traceability is also valuable for auditing purposes, as it allows an unbroken chain of documentation to be created, which ensures correct procedures are followed and additionally that production processes are correctly documented in full.

Age Control

Age control is the practice of maintaining a stock of components or products based on their age as defined by the production processes; the beginning point can be date of manufacture, date of stocking, or another point as outlined in the procedures. In an age control scheme, parts that remain in stock until the age control point is reached are removed from stock, and recycled or destroyed. The age information, often stored in batch numbers or lot numbers, is stored along with other pertinent information (such as special instructions or handling procedures if a product reaches a certain age before being used) and is part of a product traceability system.

Shelf Life

Shelf life is the period during which a component or product can remain in storage and still be considered viable. Knowing the shelf life, and from which point to begin marking the shelf life, is important for quality inspection purposes, as it allows a quality inspector to track how long a product remains usable, how often it is used, and other traits that may be useful to know for audit purposes. The shelf life information, which is often stored in batch numbers or lot numbers, is stored along with other pertinent information (such as special instructions or handling procedures if a product reaches a certain age before being used) and is part of a product traceability system.

"First-in First-out"

First-in first-out is the term applied to a common method of organizing stored components or products where the first product shelved or stored is subsequently the first product to be pulled from the shelves when a replacement or new one is needed. First-in first-out, or FIFO, is seen in multiple instances in daily life, from milk storage at the supermarket to lining up at the movie theater, and is the generally accepted methodology for storing replacements or spares in a production environment. A product traceability system, which usually includes other pertinent information (such as special instructions or handling procedures if a product reaches a certain age before being used), is usually organized on this basis.

Nonconforming Material

Material that does not conform to quality standards for a production process can have a number of potential effects. At the least, nonconforming material can lead to a part or component that is not up to standards and may fail sooner or simply not provide an adequate level of performance; at the worst, nonconforming material may lead to safety issues or hazardous conditions. As a result, quality inspectors need to make sure they can identify nonconforming material and identify proper procedures for handling, working with and/or disposing of material that does not meet quality standards. These procedures are a necessary part of any inspection planning that happens prior to implementing production processes.

Tagging

Tagging, or the practice of marking a product or component to distinguish it from others, is one of the simplest ways of identifying nonconforming material in a production process. Tagging is a binary process, most often used to flag material in a pass/fail testing environment, and can be done electronically or physically, using stickers or other visual demarcations. Although tagging generally contains the least information possible about failure or passing conditions (only marking whether a given condition is present or not), it also allows for the fastest processing, since an operator or inspector only has to search for the presence of a tag in order to make a decision about the product or component.

Labeling

Labeling is the process of attaching information about a product or component to the same product or component so that information can be read by another person or agent further along in the production process or once the product has been released. Labeling provides a greater level of information than tagging, and unlike tagging, can be used in finer gradations of decision-making and process analysis. As a result, labeling is a more complex process than tagging, and is best used in systems with a certain degree of automation, as automated systems can better handle rapid uses of label information in a production environment. The decision to use tagging or labeling should be made in the inspection planning process.

Segregating

Segregating is the process of separating items in a batch or lot based on a characteristic or set of characteristics; in a quality inspection context, this means separating items that meet quality standards from items that do not based on the aforementioned characteristics. With most modern production processes, segregation is a process that is automated, based on pre-programmed criteria that are generally defined in the inspection planning process; the decision to use segregation and what to do with segregated material is also made in the inspection planning phase. Segregation can be based on labels, tags or qualities measured in-process, making it the most complex process in the identification and handling of nonconforming material.

Product Features/Defects Classification

Classifying the features/defects of a product run can have several immediate effects on the production run and/or quality processes. Evaluation of a product's usability, analysis of the production processes to reveal flaws or bottlenecks, performing checks of the entire production run: all these and more can be done with analysis of features/defects. As with identifying nonconforming material, the classification scheme—what passes, the standard definitions, who judges what—should be identified and laid out as part of the inspection planning process. Classifying features/defects as a process is intertwined with the identification of nonconforming material, as the classification process leads to the analysis and decision-making process for something that is non-conforming.

"Critical"

In a quality inspection context, critical can have two definitions. The first definition of critical means absolutely vital, or essential; this more positive definition generally applies to features. The second definition, and the more common one for quality inspectors, is a defect that makes the product unsuitable for use, and in some cases, dangerous to attempt to use or even handle if not done properly. Generally, products with critical defects are recycled or destroyed, rather than attempt to reclaim them. Other than these definitions, there is no set threshold for what separates critical defects from lesser ones; exact definitions for a process or product will be determined by relevant laws and production standards.

"Major"

Major generally refers to a level of importance that is noteworthy, but not the showstoppers that critical features/defects are. Major defects are considered defects that lead to a loss of performance and impaired functionality, but do not carry the same weight or potential for trouble that critical defects do. Similarly, major features are important, but not considered the functionality or usability draws that critical features are. In both cases, major marks the middle ground of what is usually considered to be a three-part scale. Other than these definitions, there is no set threshold for what separates major defects from lesser ones; exact definitions for a process or product will be determined by relevant laws and production standards.

"Minor"

Minor is the lowest level of importance for both defects and features; features that are minor may not be worthy of mention in official documentation, and are certainly not considered a swaying point when considering the pros and cons of a particular product. Minor defects are those which create a general lowering of the quality of a given product, but not necessarily enough to cause the product to fail outright or even fail to meet the given quality standards. Other than these definitions, there is no set threshold for what separates minor defects from other categorizations; exact definitions for a process or product will be determined by relevant laws and production standards.

Material Review Boards

A material review board is, in a quality inspection context, a group made up of members from several different areas or sections of the production process that convenes to review production output and decide on succeeding steps should the output not meet quality standards. Based on the existing inspection plan and the board's recommendations, the disposition of nonconforming material can take several forms, ranging from scrap to reprocess to customer waiver. It is generally the board's responsibility to determine the final outcome of these materials, as well as find practical standards to which the material must be held based on the defined quality guidelines, as well as any applicable laws or regulations.

Rework

Rework is a term generally used to describe a process for remedying components or products that do not meet quality standards. When a product or component goes through the rework process, it means that the material is salvageable from its present state, and can be made to meet standards through additional labor or materials, which is what rework does. Rework is not the most extensive process for raising a product or component to standards, and because it offers the least amount of additional cost in most cases (except for certain specialized components or pieces), it is one of the most common processes used in a production environment to correct nonconforming conditions.

Reprocess

Reprocess is a term used to describe a reclamation process more extensive than reworking; during reprocess, a component or product that fails to meet quality standards is broken down into its basic components, reclaimed (sometimes destructively, depending on materials that need to be reclaimed) and sent through the production process again, creating a new product or component out of the original materials. This process is more expensive than rework, but avoids the write-off of material and time associated with destructive, non-reclaimed product disposal. Reprocessed products, unlike reworked products, are usually indistinguishable from the new models. Because of its utility and recycling of materials, reprocess is also commonly used to reclaim products or materials in a production environment.

Scrap

When something is designated scrap in a production environment, that generally means the material will be broken down or disassembled for use in either the production process or another process; it can also be sold for use by other entities or recycled. Scrap differs from reprocess in the fact that scrap material is usually not used in the same fashion or process that the original material was. For example, metal that is scrapped in a production process might be melted down and used for lesser-quality parts or different processes altogether, whereas reprocess material is turned around and used in the same production process that produced the component or material originally.

Customer Waivers

Customer waiver is an exception to the other nonconforming material methods; when customer waiver is invoked, the nonconforming material is sent along to the customer for limited or exceptional usage, along with data delineating how the material does not meet quality standards and paperwork outlining the transfer of liability to the customer. Waivers are used in situations where a customer may have use for material that does not meet normal quality standards, or the intended usage is such that normal quality standards may not be applicable. In any case, customer waiver is an exception to normal nonconforming material processes, and should be used infrequently, if any such process is in place.

Testing Methods a Quality Inspector Might Use

While there are a multitude of separate tests a quality inspector may perform, the tests themselves generally fall within one of four basic types. The first type is nondestructive testing, which generally means any test that measures properties of the product or component without disturbing or degrading the integrity or structure of the component. Non destructive testing also does not restrict the future usage of the component, unlike destructive testing, which tests properties to the failure point and renders the specimen unusable for future tests. Another type is functionality testing, which checks to ensure that the product or component both meets stated specifications for structure and performs within expected tolerances. The final type is hardness testing, which checks for the ability of the product or component to resist deformation, scarring or other physical changes made through contact that might render the product or component unusable.

X-Ray Testing

X-ray testing is a nondestructive type of testing that uses high-energy x-ray beams to examine the internal structure and composition of a product or component. Because the radiation passes right through the material, it does not affect the material composition (except in biological material, generally) and so does not change the object being tested. X-ray tests can be done using single exposures, known as film radiography, or using a monitoring system to show changes and angle shifts as they happen, known as real-time radiography. Radiography is generally used to examine structure and density variations; differences in thickness and space are easily seen in radiographic examinations, allowing for detection of cracks and other flaws.

Eddy Current Testing

Eddy current testing is a type of testing where electromagnetic fields are generated through induction and applied to materials in order to test for several properties. Eddy current testing is often used to test objects with topological complexity beyond simple shapes, and is most often used to check for minute surface flaws and conductivity issues. Because of the use of electromagnetic fields, eddy current testing can only be done on conductive materials, and can easily miss flaws below the surface or that run in a parallel direction to the field generated. However, eddy current testing is a quick and efficient way to determine several useful data points, and is a commonly used testing method.

Ultrasonic Testing

Ultrasonic testing, like x-ray testing, is a type of testing method that allows nondestructive scans of the internal structure of a product or component. Unlike x-ray, ultrasonic testing uses high-frequency vibrations to detect voids, cracks or other internal flaws or spaces in said material, which is lower-energy than x-ray, has less potential negative effects than x-rays and avoids the possibility of ionization. Ultrasonic testing is most often used in internal structure examinations and in failure analysis, particularly in components that have suffered apparent mechanical failure, although ultrasonic testing is also commonly used to determine thickness of internal materials. It is generally used on metals, though it can be applied to ceramics as well.

Dye Penetrant Testing

Dye penetrant testing is a more complex, nondestructive testing process that uses high-contrast or fluorescent dyes to seep into and highlight surface flaws in a product or component. Since it does not depend on electromagnetism, dye penetrant testing can be done on non-ferrous metals and non-metallic materials, is a highly effective method of searching surface areas for defects and does not require a lot of operator knowledge to perform correctly. However, it requires considerably more steps than other methods, as the surface must be cleaned and prepared, then cleaned again after the testing is complete, and the dyes used can be polluting; also, metal surfaces must have all finishes or glazes removed before testing can take place.

Magnetic Particle Testing

Magnetic particle testing is another testing method that uses electromagnetism to evaluate products or components for flaws or density changes; however, unlike eddy current testing, magnetic particle testing uses magnetic fields to check for changes in the magnetic resistance of an object, as defects should have far less ability to respond to magnetic fields. Magnetic particle testing can only be performed on ferrous materials, but can be used with a high degree of accuracy to detect internal manufacturing flaws or fatigue defects, as well as verifying structural details and searching out changes or voids in the structure. It is most often applied to material in the first stages of the production process and to finished products.

Tensile Testing

Tensile testing, or applying a deforming force along an axis of a material until the failure point is reached, is considered one of the simplest destructive tests that a quality inspector might perform. The objective of tensile testing is to discover the strength of the material—how much force must be applied to deform—and its failure point—how much force must be applied to break the material. Elasticity and rigidity are among the other properties that tensile testing can be used to discover. Tensile testing is most often applied to load-bearing materials such as plastic or metals, but materials that might be used for cabling (such as glass, in the case of fiber optics) are also routinely subjected to tensile testing.

Force Testing

Force testing is another common form of destructive test that is commonly found in a quality inspection environment. In force testing, a compressing force is applied to a material to determine the amount of force needed to begin deformation due to compression or tension and the amount of force needed to cause product failure, similar to tensile testing, although generally along a different axis. This type of testing is most often performed on load-bearing components like frames or pillars, connectors and joints, and pressure-related components such as tubes and pipes. Testing can be done through material compression, which can be vertical or horizontal, bending or flexing material, and the application of torque.

Leak Testing

Leak testing, or the examination of sealed components under pressure or vacuum situations to check for flaws in the sealing of the components, is a specialized form of testing. Unlike the other forms of destructive testing, leak testing must be done in a controlled environment, and thus requires more planning. Leak testing is often more subtle than other tests, as leaks do not follow prescribed patterns and are capable of developing over time. Leak testing is generally done to lower the chances of losing structural integrity, creating contamination or pollution or prematurely failing the part in a working environment. Testing is generally done with inert gases or fluids, in an environment with variable atmospheric conditions.

Tension Testing

Tension testing is very similar to tensile testing; in fact, in many cases the procedures are identical. The difference between tension testing, which is considered a functionality test, and tensile testing is that the objective of tension testing is to ensure that deformation of a material or object does not happen within the stated requirements or properties of a product. Knowing the breaking point or deformation point of a material is useful, but tension tests reveal how the material behaves under a tension force, which more closely mimics the likely working conditions of the material, which will give a clearer picture of how the material or component will behave in the real world.

Torque Testing

Torque testing is a specialized type of testing in that it measures the capacity of a product to withstand or generate torque, which is an angular force applied to alter rotational motion of a component or product. Testing for torque may involve one sub-component or the entire assembly, depending on the nature of the testing, and is often used in failure analysis, regression testing and cyclic failure testing. While the ability to deliver torque or withstand torque in disassembly is often the focus of such testing, it is also important to analyze the possibilities of angular force deforming the product or component, which is an important sub-part of torque testing.

Compression Testing

Compression testing, or the examination of materials under a compressive force (generally in alignment with gravity), has a similar relationship to force testing as tensile testing has to tension testing. When performing compression testing, the objective is to determine the general behavior of a material or component under a compressive force, not to stress it to the failure point. Knowing the breaking point or deformation point of a material is useful, but compression tests reveal how the material behaves under a crushing force, which more closely mimics the likely working conditions of the material, which will give a clearer picture of how the material or component will behave in the real world.

Hardness Tests

Hardness tests, which are designed to define a material's resistance to permanent deformation, come in many different varieties. There are four hardness tests that a quality inspector will likely perform more often, starting with the Brinell test, which defines hardness through resistance to an indenting tool loaded on a test specimen and is used to avoid surface fatigue due to repeated loads. Another common hardness test is the Rockwell test, which uses a minor and major load on indenters to express the hardness value of a material directly. The durometer test uses a presser foot and multiple scales to derive a dimensionless value; it is most commonly used on plastics and other polymer materials. Micro-hardness tests use a diamond tip to test hardness on incredibly small samples, yielding a highly accurate value that is good for a number of forces; however, it requires a microscope to use this test correctly.

Verifying Test Equipment Software

For test equipment software, there are certain basic steps that should be taken in order to verify its calibration and utility to test equipment users. The software should be safeguarded, which can mean secure, but also means that users do not access to vital components that they do not need and are protected from inadvertently accessing areas that could damage data integrity. Also, the software should include functional checks, built-in routines that act as diagnostic utilities to ensure that the software operates in the correct fashion. Test results should be compared against previous results and/or defined test outcomes; this allows the software to check against known values and evaluate if results are coming out in the general area they should. Finally, the software should be able to properly identify the attributes the test equipment is measuring and the parameters the equipment must work within.

Quality Assurance

MEAN

The mean, or arithmetic mean, of a set of numbers or values is an estimate of the center value of the set. It is calculated by adding up all the values in the set, then dividing that aggregate value by the number of values in the set. For example, if you needed to find the mean of the set of numbers {25, 50, 24, 26, 35, 20}, you would add them together—25+50+24+26+30+20=180—then divide the result by the number of values. In this case, 180/6=30, so the mean of the set of numbers {25, 50, 24, 26, 35, 20} would be 30. Notice that the mean is not related to the distribution of the numbers; it simply refers to the value that is at the numeric center of the listed values.

MEDIAN

The median of a set of numbers or values is the value which occupies the center point of the set, at which half of the set is of greater numeric value than the center point and half the set is of lesser numeric value. This differs from the mean, which is the actual center value; what this translates to is that the median is unaffected by having outsized values included in the set. For example, with the set of numbers {25, 50, 24, 26, 35, 20}, the median of the set can be derived by ordering the numbers in the set, and taking the middle value (if there is an odd number of values in the set) or averaging the two middle values, so if the set is properly ordered as {20, 24, 25, 26, 35, 50), the media would be (25+26)/2, which is 2.5.

MODE

In a set of numbers, the mode is the value that occurs most often in the set. Unlike the median or mean, the mode does not have to be a unique value; there can be multiple modes in a given set. For example, with the set of numbers {6, 8, 9, 11, 21, 11, 7}, the mode is 11, because it occurs twice and all the other numbers occur once. Mode can only be measured in a set with at least one repeating value; sets with no repeating value, such as a continuous distribution, need to have the data broken down into small pieces in order to create discrete intervals, which can then be used to find the mode.

RANGE

Range, often considered a measure of dispersion, or variation within a data set, is the span of values covered in a given data set. It can be determined simply by subtracting the lowest value in the data set from the highest; the result is the range. Range can also be thought of as the smallest possible interval or data set that contains all the data values. When doing statistical computations, it is helpful to know the range so that the degree of variability (or the potential number of outcomes using the given data set), as well as best-case and worst-case values, can be computed with an acceptable level of accuracy.

STANDARD DEVIATION

The standard deviation of a given data set is the value of the variation from the average value of the measurement set, mathematically defined as the square root of the population variance. It can also be thought of as the measure of how the frequency distribution is spread across the data set. In a traditional distribution curve, roughly 2/3 of the values will fall within a range of two standard deviations centered on the mean, i.e. most of the values (in practice, about 68%) will be within one standard deviation below the mean or one standard deviation above it, and about 95% will be within two standard deviations of the mean one way or the other.

Review Video: Standard Deviation
Visit mometrix.com/academy and enter code: 419469

Variance

Variance is a measure of how far from the mean or arithmetic mean the values of a data set are dispersed; it is a measure of the values relative to the mean, not where they might be expected to sit. The formula for determining variance depends on whether the variance being computed is for an entire population of data or a sample of the data set, but is dependent on the squared deviations in both cases. The relationship between variance and distance of individual values from the mean is a direct one, and is also dependent on the number of degrees of freedom in the observations of the data set.

Proportion or Percentage Calculations

The use of percentages, even with multiple data sets, is a less complex operation than tests for proportion. Percentages are derived by dividing the data set into 100 equal subsets, and then tallying the applicable subsets relative to the total number of 100; even over multiple sets, the principle remains simple. Tests for proportion are more complex; for one thing, the standard deviation for proportions, which must be calculated for statistically significant operations, is defined as the square root of $p(1-p)/n$, where p is the population proportion and n represents sample size. The resulting distribution that is calculable is binomial, meaning two variables are expressed; in this case, in terms of n and p, i.e. mean is the product of n and p, and variance is the product of the mean and $(1-p)$.

Histograms

A histogram is, in a statistical context, a special type of graphical display. Histograms show frequency distributions in bar graph form, displaying the data on a two-axis graph with colored or shaded bars to represent the data points in a set relative to the defined axes on the graph. Unlike other forms of bar graphs, histograms are continuous, so that the lower edge of one displayed interval is the upper edge of another and so on, and their bars touch as part of the continuous nature of their display. Since histograms display frequency distribution data, one axis of the graph is always a measurement of time (generally the horizontal axis, but not always).

Scatter Diagrams

Scatter diagrams are another form of graphical display that illustrates the relationship between two variables. These diagrams generally show correlation patterns, but not a causative one, meaning scatter diagrams do not show a cause-and-effect relationship between the plotted variables. Scatter diagrams are, like most of the statistical graphic displays, two-dimensional in nature, framing the variables along an x- and y-axis. The axes can be labeled as any number of potential attributes, including time; since causative relationships are not expressed in scatter diagrams, however, time does not have to be one of the defined axes. The correlative relationships are generally direct as expressed in the diagrams; however, the dual-variable nature of the diagram does not allow for the possible influence of other, unplotted variables.

Tally Sheets

Tally sheets are a simpler form of graphical display that generally illustrates the raw data in a set of data points; they can be organized with the questions or attributes that generated the data, or be a simple table. Tally sheets differ from other graphical displays in that they show the data before any type of analysis or reorganization has been performed; this makes relationships less obvious when examining them, but can be useful if there is reason to suspect the validity of a relationship or conclusion about the data. Tally sheets are often considered the basic form of the data set, and are thus extremely useful as a primary resource and/or a check on any data analysis that is performed upon the set(s).

Bar Charts

Bar charts are similar in appearance to histograms, and are often used for similar purposes: displaying frequency distribution data. However, bar charts differ in that they are not continuous displays—meaning the bars do not touch—and are generally rotated 90º from histograms. However, this is only a general practice, and is not an indicator one way or the other. Bar charts are most commonly used to display financial data, although the two-dimensional graph formula for graphical displays can be used for many types of data relationships. Unlike histograms, bar charts do not always display data in relationship to time, and so are capable of displaying other variables besides chronology.

Normal Distribution

A normal distribution is a standard arrangement of data points that provides an equal chance of any randomly chosen data point to be above or below the mean of the data set. The normal distribution is the touchstone of most statistical analysis; graphically, it is represented by a bell curve, a continuous curve that rises from the x-axis to a point representing the mean on the y-axis, then curves down to approach the x-axis again. This bell curve is symmetrical around the mean, which means that the curves are the same on both sides, and demonstrate a clustering of data points around the mean, with the frequency becoming more and sparser as the curve proceeds further away. Roughly 2/3 of the values (in practice, about 68%) will be within one standard deviation of the mean, and about 95% will be within two standard deviations of the mean.

Statistical Process Control

Statistical process control (SPC) is a term to describe the general methodology of using statistical methods and techniques to modify and control a production process, keeping the process and its output within predefined parameters through action based on statistical analysis, including distribution analysis, data pattern mining and tolerance reviews. One of the primary purposes of SPC is to reduce variation in the output and process, thus making the process more robust and resistant to variation of sub-processes due to mechanical wear, environmental conditions and myriad other real-world factors. SPC is invaluable from a quality inspection standpoint, because it is ultimately focused on quality control, which makes it simpler for inspectors to verify and investigate quality issues.

Causes of Variation

In a statistical process control (SPC) environment, certain factors are taken into account during the analysis phase. These factors can be predicted based on the process and the nature of the system, such as mechanical wear, maintenance cycles, environmental changes and human error, and are known statistical factors. These factors are known as common causes of variation, because they and their general effects on a process can be predicted with a fair degree of accuracy, and are considered inside statistical control for this reason. Special causes of variation, on the other hand, are less subject to analytic inclusion because they are unusual or have effects beyond what statistical analysis can forecast. Special causes would include major accidents, natural disasters or rapid market shifts, and can at best be loosely approximated in SPC modeling, putting them outside of statistical control.

"Run"

When analyzing data patterns, a run is a continuous sequence of events of the same occurrence in a data set of observations; it can also be a consecutive series of increasing or decreasing measurements in a set of variable values. Depending on the application, a run can be defined by as many as five points plotted or observed consecutively, especially if three of those points fall outside the predefined tolerance markers for the process. However, the importance of the run is contained in its consecutive nature, because consecutive events may indicate an area of concern or further investigation in a production process, particularly if the run is not accounted for by present statistical models.

"Trend"

Trends are similar to runs in a statistical process control sense, in that they both represent consecutive series of events that stand out from the data set. Trends, however, are longer-lasting than runs—generally, a trend is considered to be seven or more data points in a continuously upward or downward direction—and are of more import; a run may indicate an area of concern or not, but a trend represents an alteration in the process, and needs to be investigated. Trends can be caused by natural evolutions or changes in the process, but when they appear, trends need to be managed at the minimum, for better output control and resource management.

"Hugging"

Hugging is where a distribution of data points is clustered around a data value other than the mean of the set. Generally hugging follows the same rule of thumb as runs and trends do numerically, meaning five or less is a run, whereas seven or more would be a trend, but it differs in that there isn't an ascending or descending direction to the clustering. Hugging is often caused by faulty sample selection in testing; if the testing is done such that a truly random selection is not achieved, the data values can be skewed and as a result cause the resultant points to cluster or hug a certain value. Like the appearance of runs or trends, hugging should be investigated when noticed, to ensure the process shift, if present, remains under the process control set up by the process owner.

Action Responses to Analysis

After data analysis is done, generally accepted good management practices call for one of a handful of general actions. The first, and most common, of these actions would be to take remedial action to fix the direct problem identified by the analysis and subsequent investigation. After the issue is fixed, the next action to take would be to perform a root cause analysis of the issue; this identifies what caused the issue, and helps identify what steps could be taken to prevent a reoccurrence. Finally, if necessary, the last action would be to perform a preventative action that will keep the issue from reoccurring or prevent the issue from spreading in scope.

Control and Specification Limits

Control limits and specification limits are similar concepts in construction, but are different in how they are applied. Control limits are boundaries for deviations from the central line on a control chart, and are defined by process data only; they mark out-of-boundary conditions that a process reaches, and are of greater use on the planning and inspection side. Specification limits, on the other hand, can be defined in a number of ways, but are generally boundaries for deviation based on specific attributes on an item-by-item basis, rather than subgroups like control limits; these limits can be set by different parties in the process, even the end-user or consumer in some cases. Specification limits are used in quality assessment, whereas control limits are used in process assessment.

XBAR–R CHARTS

Xbar charts are control charts—graphs that help track a process against defined standards and error conditions and demonstrate if the process is in statistical control—that demonstrate changes in the mean value of the overall process. An xbar-R chart is a more specialized version that displays both the mean value and the range of the sample being tested, generally using the maximum and minimum values in the range as bounds for the graph. This allows a user to focus on specific intervals in the data output of the process, and is very useful for checking on both mean values and distribution simultaneously. Xbar-R charts are commonly used to check for abnormalities in the process run.

XBAR-S CHARTS

An xbar-s chart is another specialized version of a control chart. In virtually all respects, xbar-s charts are identical to xbar-R charts, except that xbar-s charts track the mean of a process and the standard deviation chart. The displays are virtually identical in structure. Xbar-s charts are recommended for use when the logical group size of the sample is larger than 10, as xbar-R charts can become unwieldy with larger logical groups. Xbar-s charts are generally more useful for tracking process shifts and as a back check for control limit definitions than actual issues with the run itself, although dispersion issues in the frequency distribution can be seen in much finer scale when using xbar-s charts.

P-CHARTS

A p-chart is a version of an attribute chart, a version of a control chart designed to display data relating to specific attributes of a data set. In the case of the p-chart, it is designed to display the percentage of samples that display a specific attribute. The chart is valid for sample sizes that are fixed or varying, and shows the percentage of samples that do not have the attribute as well. P-charts are structurally very similar to xbar charts, except that the attribute proportion is the basis of the chart rather than the sample mean. Before compiling a p-chart, the nonconforming standard must be clearly delineated in order to derive statistically valid measurements.

NP-CHARTS

An np-chart is another version of an attribute chart. In the case of the np-chart, it is designed to display the incidence of samples that display a specific attribute over a given interval or distribution. With np-charts, the chart is only valid for sample sizes that are constant in size, and as part of the main purpose of the chart, shows the percentage of samples that do not have the attribute as well. Np-charts are structurally very similar to xbar charts, except that the attribute occurrence is the basis of the chart rather than the sample mean. Because np-charts are concerned only with occurrences, as opposed to nonconforming conditions, np-charts are somewhat simpler to compile and read.

C-CHARTS

A c-chart can be considered a specialized version of an np-chart. C-charts are designed to display the incidence of samples that display a specific attribute over a given interval or distribution, but unlike np-charts, c-charts are valid for samples than can have more than one incidence of the given attribute. Like np-charts, the chart is only valid for sample sizes that are constant in size, and as part of the main purpose of the chart, shows the percentage of samples that do not have the attribute as well. C-charts are structurally very similar to xbar charts, except that the attribute frequency is the basis of the chart rather than the sample mean. Due to the possibility of multiple occurrences of attributes possible per sample with c-charts, they are more complex than np-charts.

U-Charts

A u-chart can be considered a specialized version of a p-chart. U-charts are designed to display the percentage of samples that display a specific attribute over a given interval or distribution, but unlike p-charts, u-charts are valid for samples than can have more than one incidence of the given attribute. U-charts are, like p-charts, valid for sample sizes of constant or variable size. As with the other attribute charts, u-charts are structurally very similar to xbar charts; however, attribute occurrence is the basis of the chart rather than the sample mean. Due to the possibility of multiple occurrences of attributes possible per sample with u-charts, they are more complex than p-charts.

Process Capability Analysis

In essence, process capability analysis compares how a process performs its assigned tasks against the pre-defined specifications for that process. If all or nearly all variables in the process are within the specification, the process is said to be capable. Process capability itself is considered to be the range of variance for a characteristic or set of characteristics for a product; in practical terms, it can be defined as the best overall performance of the process over a set of operations that meet specifications. Analysis of this capability involves multiple indexes and data aggregations, and is expressed mathematically as six times the sample standard deviation of the process when it is in a state of statistical control.

C_P

C_p, also known as the process capability index, is a measure of the capability of a process in relation to a specific attribute over the reference interval of the process, which follows the standard definition as being bounded by the 99.865% fractile on the upper bound and the 0.135% fractile on the lower bound. C_p is measured only for a process in statistical control—another index measurement is used for non-statistical control processes, which is covered in another flashcard—and is defined mathematically as the difference between the upper specification limit and the lower specification limit, divided by the process capability, which is six times the sample standard deviation of the process.

C_{PK}

C_{pk} is an expression of the minimum process capability index, which is defined as the smaller of two process capability indexes: the upper process capability index and the lower process capability index. Calculating C_{pk} is useful for determining the lower bound of acceptability for a process, as well as maintaining a baseline for statistical control. Mathematically, the indexes are defined as follows:

- Upper process capability index—The difference between the upper specification limit and the process average, divided by three times the sample standard deviation (i.e. half the process capability)
- Lower process capability index—The difference between the process average and the lower specification limit, divided by three times the sample standard deviation.

P_P

P_p, also known as the process performance index, is a measure of a process outcome with respect to a specific attribute when the process may or may not be in a state of statistical control. In order to provide a more effective definition, the performance itself is measured against a specified tolerance. Mathematically, P_p is defined as the difference between the upper specification limit and the lower specification limit, divided by six times the standard deviation; process capability is not applicable, since any performance index must take into account the potential presence of both random and special causes of variation, which the definition of process capability as provided in another flashcard cannot do.

P_{PK}

P_{pk} is an expression of the minimum process performance index, which is defined as the smaller of two process performance indexes: the upper process performance index and the lower process performance index. Calculating P_{pk} is useful for determining the lower bound of acceptability for process functionality, as well as maintaining a baseline for statistical control. Mathematically, the indexes are defined as follows:

- Upper process performance index—The difference between the upper specification limit and the process mean, divided by three times the standard deviation. This definition is only valid for a symmetrical normal distribution.
- Lower process performance index—The difference between the process mean and the lower specification limit, divided by three times the standard deviation.

Quality Improvement

Quality improvement can be defined in a number of ways depending on the terminology of the user, but the essence of quality improvement is to improve the performance of a process or organization. Another way to look at this, and a more accurate way from a quality inspection standpoint, is that quality improvement is a system designed to minimize variability, or changes, in a process and the resulting output of the process, i.e. products. An effective quality improvement system integrates several concepts and approaches, from planning to manufacturing to customer service and feedback, and organizes these approaches into a unified system of managed responses to various quality issues arising in a production process.

Prevention vs Detection

From a quality standpoint, prevention vs. detection is one of the central concepts of quality improvement. It refers to issues of design as opposed to remedial action, and reflects a complementary approach to quality preservation and improvement. Prevention means designing features into a process or product that keeps non-conforming events or measurements from taking place; this takes place in the planning and designing stage. Detection, on the other hand, means inspecting a process or product for non-conforming events or measurements and taking palliative action based on what is discovered, which happens in the manufacturing or inspection stage. Both approaches are necessary to create and maintain quality, but they are fundamentally different ways to approach a quality question.

Customer Satisfaction

The idea of customer satisfaction is a nebulous one for quality inspectors many times, since quality inspection is focused on processes and products, not what happens after the products leave for the consumer world. However, customers are what drive an enterprise, and the entire concept of quality is based in part on customer expectations and perceptions. Repeated studies have found that customer satisfaction is a key to maintaining a successful business for a number of reasons: dissatisfied customers tell more people about their experience than satisfied ones do, the costs of bringing in new customers are far higher than keeping existing ones, profitability is far easier to reach with happy customers, and so on. Thus, customer satisfaction is arguably the reason for quality inspection, and thus needs to be preserved.

Poor Quality

Poor quality has a number of components, not all of which can easily be tallied. Directly, the following components can be counted when trying to compute the total cost of poor quality (COPQ):

- Cost of the labor of operators, technicians, and other employees necessary to rectify the quality issues
- Cost of the materials needed to correct or redo the product or process
- Overhead that goes into the process, including ancillary production costs like utilities
- Loss of sale share based on lower yield of process or product

Indirect costs are more difficult to compute, but may be equally or even more costly. These costs include loss of momentum in the marketplace, lost faith in the company on the part of consumers, and reluctance to consider company in future buying decisions. These costs are not reported directly or even perceived directly, but they can have long-lasting consequences.

Total Quality Management

Total quality management (TQM) is a system of management that aims to improve quality by realigning all levels of a process or organization to focus on quality as a primary mission instead of a sidebar to specific tasks. Under the precepts of TQM, quality will arise when an organization focuses on a handful of primary concepts, including continuous process improvement and customer focus; much of TQM is derived from Japanese management styles, which is traditionally less product-focused than Western management styles. From a quality inspection standpoint, TQM includes a great deal of statistical analysis and root-cause investigations, as well as an impressive array of tests designed to maximize usable data for quality and design purposes.

Product vs Process

Although many of the operations and concepts a quality inspector works with can be applied to products and processes, products are not synonymous with processes. A process is a connected series of operations and resources that are designed to function together and produce a set output from input materials and information. A product, on the other hand, is simply the outcome of a process, which is generally a defined service or physical object. Processes generally involve physical actions, but are not in and of themselves physical objects, whereas products generally are, although processes are frequently given graphical representation as flowcharts, which are hierarchical drawings that delineate inputs, outputs and intermediate steps in varying degrees of detail.

Manufacturing Relationships

Every piece of an end-to-end process has an effect on the other pieces. For example, the design of a product will define the processes used to manufacture it, as some processes will not be able to handle scale or precision to whatever degree the product requires. Additionally, the design will also affect what goes into the product, as some materials may require environmental extremes to use safely, which may not be possible with some processes. This relationship works in both directions; if a certain process must be used, it will affect the initial design of the product, and if a certain type of material is required, it will affect the processes and design to be used. The type of output that must be achieved will decide the previous steps (design, material, process) as well; again, this relationship is two-way, depending on what aspects carry the highest priority.

External vs Internal Audit

From a quality standpoint, external and internal audits have a lot of similarities. External audits are an organized review and investigation of an organization's processes and procedures, performed by an unaffiliated outside organization, in order to evaluate and offer guidance on improving quality control and management. Internal audits are identical in focus and intent; the only substantial difference is that internal audits are carried out by an independent, objective part of the organization itself, rather than pulling in an outside entity. Internal audits can be more effective due to the ease of working within an existing structure and familiarity with standard procedures, but external audits sometimes carry more weight with customers, as well as offering the ability to have a different perspective.

Audit Types

Among the many different labels audits are given are: system, product and process audits. System audits and process audits are often used interchangeably as terms used to describe reviews of any activity, often using a certain document or set of documents as a baseline, such as an administrator manual or defined procedure set. However, while the definition holds true for process audits, system audits can also refer to reviews and investigations of entire systems, such as information systems, which can encompass an entire set of processes. Product audits are generally simpler in scale, being a review of a specific product or service against its stated specifications and objectives to determine how well a product or service meets its own stated goals and specifications, i.e. determining the product or service's fitness for use.

Corrective Action Requests

Corrective action requests are one of the most vital pieces of quality improvement, because they often serve as the engine for improvement. A corrective action request (CAR) is essentially a request by a process user or entity to address and repair at the root level a condition that either is or causes a non-conforming event or state of events in a process or product. CARs are vital because they provide a channel of communication between entities invested in a process, and make those with authority over processes aware of issues that may not be visible from an administrative level, but may cause any number of issues at midrange or lower levels of the process. From a TQM standpoint, CARs are even more important, because they reinforce the idea that quality is the responsibility of all invested process members, not just those in charge.

Quality Control Tools

The seven tools of quality control all figure into statistical analysis quite heavily. These tools are:

- Checksheet—Used to present data in an efficient fashion, often as a list.
- Pareto chart—Used to display the event count data in decreasing order, highlighting the factors with the highest aggregate effect on a system.
- Flowchart—Used to break a process down into a graphical representation of the constituent steps.
- Ishikawa (cause and effect) diagram—Used to connect multiple possible causes to a single observed effect, outlining causal relationships in a logical, legible fashion.
- Histogram—Used to provide simple graphical view of distribution and central tendency of data.

- Scatter diagram—Used to provide graphical view of data points interrelationships across variables
- Control chart—Used to demonstrate the variation range of a system and demonstrate if a process is in or out of normal function

Plan-Do Study-Act/Plan-Do Check-Act Cycle

The plan-do study-act/plan-do check-act (PDSA/PDCA) cycle, also known as the Deming cycle after the famous statistician who developed the cycle into its present form, is a continuous process improvement initiative that takes the form of a repetitive step-by-step procedure to refine and improve the quality of a process or system. The steps are:

- Plan—Make forecasts for change, then analyze the forecasts against past trends. Predict possible futures and create a plan based on those forecasts.
- Do—Implement the plan, taking action in minute, easily controlled steps under controlled conditions.
- Study (Check)—Analyze the results of the plan.
- Act—Based on the results, refine the process or implement improvements.

Six Sigma DMAIC ethodology

The business improvement system known as Six Sigma, originally developed by Motorola, has two primary methodologies that are used to remove defects from processes and thereby raise quality. Of the two, the DMAIC methodology is more commonly used from a quality inspection perspective. The steps in the DMAIC methodology are:

- Define—Lay out process improvement objectives, based on business needs, overall strategy and customer demands.
- Measure—Take values for present processes and subsequent data points for use in system revision and for historical purposes.
- Analyze—Review processes and data to determine causality, interrelationships between variables, and to ensure all valid factors have been included.
- Improve—Take results of analysis and use to apply revisions to process.
- Control—Create test runs in order to correct for variations before introducing into production, then measure process and install mechanisms for oversight and correction.

Root Cause Analysis

Root cause analysis is a vital point of quality improvement, although often a not-pleasant one. Root cause analysis is the study of the causative factors behind variations in a process or products, or in simpler terms, the analysis of consequences and the act of learning from them. This analysis begins with an examination of the individual processes that are part of the overall train of events, then reviews the nexus points of decisions or control actions and determines the chain of reasoning that led to those decisions and works to determine what options existed at that point and the possible outcomes of alternate decision paths. Through this analysis and feedback to process owners, alternative courses of action are discovered and implemented for future occurrences, thereby reducing variations and improving quality.

Safety Data Sheets

Safety Data Sheets (SDS) are important safety tools; they provide information on chemical agents, including name, composition, proper handling techniques, first aid procedures, personal protection procedures, toxicological data and other safety-related data. By international law, all organizations that use potentially hazardous chemicals—which can range from cleaning alcohol to industrial acids—must maintain the applicable SDS where employees and official inspectors can view them if needed. From a quality inspection standpoint, SDS are necessary to have on hand because they play a factor in different quality processes, including emergency response procedures and production processes, as well as safety procedures mandated by the requisite organization (in the United States, that organization is the Occupational Safety and Health Administration).

Personal Protective Equipment

Personal protective equipment, or any devices or clothing designed to shield people from the toxic or hazardous effects of environmental hazards, is a vital part of following proper safety procedures in a production environment. Depending on the type of processes that are performed in the production environment and what is listed in the SDS—the source of information about environmental hazards and the proper type of equipment to use—the types of equipment on hand might vary. Some common types of personal protective equipment include:

- Respirators—For use in fires and chemical vapor escapes.
- Gloves—For use in handling high-temperature or corrosive materials.
- Goggles—For protecting the eyes from particulate matter, chemical splashes or vapors.

Reference Documents

Quality inspectors will use many different sets of reference documents on the job, but some will come into play more often than others. The majority of documents will be supplied from the following sources:

- ISO—International Standards Organization: Maintains global standards for industrial technology, auditing and quality maintenance. Works in conjunction with the United Nations.
- ANSI—American National Standards Institute: The national (for the US) body that develops and maintains technology standards. Member of the ISO.
- ASTM—American Society for Testing Materials: Develops and establishes national testing standards for processes, materials and systems.
- QS—Quality System: May be defined by ISO or ANSI standards, but is the system in place at the organization performing audit or review. Provides specialized reference base.
- Customer requirements—Customer's needs translated into the technical specifications; scope of authority process owners have in addressing or reporting quality issues is included.

Technical Reports

Technical reports, or formal documents that provide detailed information about an issue or process in a production environment, are an invaluable tool to quality inspectors. The primary use of a technical report is to summarize and provide information on problems and their diagnoses; this is important because it allows both a historical perspective to be built concerning a process, and also because it provides information with which immediate solutions can be developed. Another important use of technical reports, and one that is generally the focus of the report, is communicating solutions to process issues to the process owners and other invested entities. An inspector must be able to read and interpret the report—generally requiring familiarity with the physical and logical details of the processes, products and material involved, as well as statistical techniques—and generate reports in order to provide the findings in intelligible fashion.

Empowering Employees

In recent years, empowering employees has become of greater interest to organizations, because it has become clear that employees who feel invested in their organization and who feel capable of making change when and where needed not only perform better, they have an overall positive effect on quality. As a result, organizations have been empowering employees by providing them with increased responsibility, making all employees active partners in quality initiatives, and forming project teams to have employees take a hand in designing and creating products and processes from the ground up. Also, some organizations, realizing the constant need for updating products and services in a modern economy, have used employees in improvement teams, leveraging existing product and company knowledge into real changes and improvements.

Team Formation Roles

When forming a team for process development or investigation, certain steps are necessary to forming an effective and workable team. Although they do not have to follow in a rigid order, they do need to be followed in order to work optimally. The first step is to select team participants, based (optimally) on skill sets, personality, teamwork ability and investedness in goal of team. Once the team is selected, the establishment of goals—within the team and for the team—and establishing the team roles must be done. A leadership structure must be set up, as well as accountability for the assigned roles and a set of ground rules for team operation and interaction. If need be, training on team functioning should be provided, along with establishing resource lines, support within the team and, most importantly, viable communication between team members.

Team Development Stages

The most common model for developing functional team dynamics is a four-stage process called forming-storming-norming-performing. Developed in 1965, it has been a popular method of building teams in multiple forums. The four stages are:

- Forming—Drawing team members in, having them meet and learn about the objectives and pertinent information about the reason for building the team.
- Storming—The most obviously Darwinian stage, where ideas are tossed out into public discussion, roles are assigned and hierarchies are developed. Often seen as the toughest stage.
- Norming—Teamwork truly begins to develop here. Collaborative work habits are developed, and the groundwork is laid for the team's real tasks. Ground rules are created.
- Performing—The team, having learned to function together and depend on each other, begins the actual work of developing solutions and approaches. Work is done as a complete unit instead of a collection of individuals.

How to Overcome Test Anxiety

Just the thought of taking a test is enough to make most people a little nervous. A test is an important event that can have a long-term impact on your future, so it's important to take it seriously and it's natural to feel anxious about performing well. But just because anxiety is normal, that doesn't mean that it's helpful in test taking, or that you should simply accept it as part of your life. Anxiety can have a variety of effects. These effects can be mild, like making you feel slightly nervous, or severe, like blocking your ability to focus or remember even a simple detail.

If you experience test anxiety—whether severe or mild—it's important to know how to beat it. To discover this, first you need to understand what causes test anxiety.

Causes of Test Anxiety

While we often think of anxiety as an uncontrollable emotional state, it can actually be caused by simple, practical things. One of the most common causes of test anxiety is that a person does not feel adequately prepared for their test. This feeling can be the result of many different issues such as poor study habits or lack of organization, but the most common culprit is time management. Starting to study too late, failing to organize your study time to cover all of the material, or being distracted while you study will mean that you're not well prepared for the test. This may lead to cramming the night before, which will cause you to be physically and mentally exhausted for the test. Poor time management also contributes to feelings of stress, fear, and hopelessness as you realize you are not well prepared but don't know what to do about it.

Other times, test anxiety is not related to your preparation for the test but comes from unresolved fear. This may be a past failure on a test, or poor performance on tests in general. It may come from comparing yourself to others who seem to be performing better or from the stress of living up to expectations. Anxiety may be driven by fears of the future—how failure on this test would affect your educational and career goals. These fears are often completely irrational, but they can still negatively impact your test performance.

Elements of Test Anxiety

As mentioned earlier, test anxiety is considered to be an emotional state, but it has physical and mental components as well. Sometimes you may not even realize that you are suffering from test anxiety until you notice the physical symptoms. These can include trembling hands, rapid heartbeat, sweating, nausea, and tense muscles. Extreme anxiety may lead to fainting or vomiting. Obviously, any of these symptoms can have a negative impact on testing. It is important to recognize them as soon as they begin to occur so that you can address the problem before it damages your performance.

The mental components of test anxiety include trouble focusing and inability to remember learned information. During a test, your mind is on high alert, which can help you recall information and stay focused for an extended period of time. However, anxiety interferes with your mind's natural processes, causing you to blank out, even on the questions you know well. The strain of testing during anxiety makes it difficult to stay focused, especially on a test that may take several hours. Extreme anxiety can take a huge mental toll, making it difficult not only to recall test information but even to understand the test questions or pull your thoughts together.

Effects of Test Anxiety

Test anxiety is like a disease—if left untreated, it will get progressively worse. Anxiety leads to poor performance, and this reinforces the feelings of fear and failure, which in turn lead to poor performances on subsequent tests. It can grow from a mild nervousness to a crippling condition. If allowed to progress, test anxiety can have a big impact on your schooling, and consequently on your future.

Test anxiety can spread to other parts of your life. Anxiety on tests can become anxiety in any stressful situation, and blanking on a test can turn into panicking in a job situation. But fortunately, you don't have to let anxiety rule your testing and determine your grades. There are a number of relatively simple steps you can take to move past anxiety and function normally on a test and in the rest of life.

Physical Steps for Beating Test Anxiety

While test anxiety is a serious problem, the good news is that it can be overcome. It doesn't have to control your ability to think and remember information. While it may take time, you can begin taking steps today to beat anxiety.

Just as your first hint that you may be struggling with anxiety comes from the physical symptoms, the first step to treating it is also physical. Rest is crucial for having a clear, strong mind. If you are tired, it is much easier to give in to anxiety. But if you establish good sleep habits, your body and mind will be ready to perform optimally, without the strain of exhaustion. Additionally, sleeping well helps you to retain information better, so you're more likely to recall the answers when you see the test questions.

Getting good sleep means more than going to bed on time. It's important to allow your brain time to relax. Take study breaks from time to time so it doesn't get overworked, and don't study right before bed. Take time to rest your mind before trying to rest your body, or you may find it difficult to fall asleep.

Along with sleep, other aspects of physical health are important in preparing for a test. Good nutrition is vital for good brain function. Sugary foods and drinks may give a burst of energy but this burst is followed by a crash, both physically and emotionally. Instead, fuel your body with protein and vitamin-rich foods.

Also, drink plenty of water. Dehydration can lead to headaches and exhaustion, especially if your brain is already under stress from the rigors of the test. Particularly if your test is a long one, drink water during the breaks. And if possible, take an energy-boosting snack to eat between sections.

Along with sleep and diet, a third important part of physical health is exercise. Maintaining a steady workout schedule is helpful, but even taking 5-minute study breaks to walk can help get your blood pumping faster and clear your head. Exercise also releases endorphins, which contribute to a positive feeling and can help combat test anxiety.

When you nurture your physical health, you are also contributing to your mental health. If your body is healthy, your mind is much more likely to be healthy as well. So take time to rest, nourish your body with healthy food and water, and get moving as much as possible. Taking these physical steps will make you stronger and more able to take the mental steps necessary to overcome test anxiety.

Mental Steps for Beating Test Anxiety

Working on the mental side of test anxiety can be more challenging, but as with the physical side, there are clear steps you can take to overcome it. As mentioned earlier, test anxiety often stems from lack of preparation, so the obvious solution is to prepare for the test. Effective studying may be the most important weapon you have for beating test anxiety, but you can and should employ several other mental tools to combat fear.

First, boost your confidence by reminding yourself of past success—tests or projects that you aced. If you're putting as much effort into preparing for this test as you did for those, there's no reason you should expect to fail here. Work hard to prepare; then trust your preparation.

Second, surround yourself with encouraging people. It can be helpful to find a study group, but be sure that the people you're around will encourage a positive attitude. If you spend time with others who are anxious or cynical, this will only contribute to your own anxiety. Look for others who are motivated to study hard from a desire to succeed, not from a fear of failure.

Third, reward yourself. A test is physically and mentally tiring, even without anxiety, and it can be helpful to have something to look forward to. Plan an activity following the test, regardless of the outcome, such as going to a movie or getting ice cream.

When you are taking the test, if you find yourself beginning to feel anxious, remind yourself that you know the material. Visualize successfully completing the test. Then take a few deep, relaxing breaths and return to it. Work through the questions carefully but with confidence, knowing that you are capable of succeeding.

Developing a healthy mental approach to test taking will also aid in other areas of life. Test anxiety affects more than just the actual test—it can be damaging to your mental health and even contribute to depression. It's important to beat test anxiety before it becomes a problem for more than testing.

Study Strategy

Being prepared for the test is necessary to combat anxiety, but what does being prepared look like? You may study for hours on end and still not feel prepared. What you need is a strategy for test prep. The next few pages outline our recommended steps to help you plan out and conquer the challenge of preparation.

Step 1: Scope Out the Test

Learn everything you can about the format (multiple choice, essay, etc.) and what will be on the test. Gather any study materials, course outlines, or sample exams that may be available. Not only will this help you to prepare, but knowing what to expect can help to alleviate test anxiety.

Step 2: Map Out the Material

Look through the textbook or study guide and make note of how many chapters or sections it has. Then divide these over the time you have. For example, if a book has 15 chapters and you have five days to study, you need to cover three chapters each day. Even better, if you have the time, leave an extra day at the end for overall review after you have gone through the material in depth.

If time is limited, you may need to prioritize the material. Look through it and make note of which sections you think you already have a good grasp on, and which need review. While you are studying, skim quickly through the familiar sections and take more time on the challenging parts.

Write out your plan so you don't get lost as you go. Having a written plan also helps you feel more in control of the study, so anxiety is less likely to arise from feeling overwhelmed at the amount to cover.

Step 3: Gather Your Tools

Decide what study method works best for you. Do you prefer to highlight in the book as you study and then go back over the highlighted portions? Or do you type out notes of the important information? Or is it helpful to make flashcards that you can carry with you? Assemble the pens, index cards, highlighters, post-it notes, and any other materials you may need so you won't be distracted by getting up to find things while you study.

If you're having a hard time retaining the information or organizing your notes, experiment with different methods. For example, try color-coding by subject with colored pens, highlighters, or post-it notes. If you learn better by hearing, try recording yourself reading your notes so you can listen while in the car, working out, or simply sitting at your desk. Ask a friend to quiz you from your flashcards, or try teaching someone the material to solidify it in your mind.

Step 4: Create Your Environment

It's important to avoid distractions while you study. This includes both the obvious distractions like visitors and the subtle distractions like an uncomfortable chair (or a too-comfortable couch that makes you want to fall asleep). Set up the best study environment possible: good lighting and a comfortable work area. If background music helps you focus, you may want to turn it on, but otherwise keep the room quiet. If you are using a computer to take notes, be sure you don't have any other windows open, especially applications like social media, games, or anything else that could distract you. Silence your phone and turn off notifications. Be sure to keep water close by so you stay hydrated while you study (but avoid unhealthy drinks and snacks).

Also, take into account the best time of day to study. Are you freshest first thing in the morning? Try to set aside some time then to work through the material. Is your mind clearer in the afternoon or evening? Schedule your study session then. Another method is to study at the same time of day that you will take the test, so that your brain gets used to working on the material at that time and will be ready to focus at test time.

Step 5: Study!

Once you have done all the study preparation, it's time to settle into the actual studying. Sit down, take a few moments to settle your mind so you can focus, and begin to follow your study plan. Don't give in to distractions or let yourself procrastinate. This is your time to prepare so you'll be ready to fearlessly approach the test. Make the most of the time and stay focused.

Of course, you don't want to burn out. If you study too long you may find that you're not retaining the information very well. Take regular study breaks. For example, taking five minutes out of every hour to walk briskly, breathing deeply and swinging your arms, can help your mind stay fresh.

As you get to the end of each chapter or section, it's a good idea to do a quick review. Remind yourself of what you learned and work on any difficult parts. When you feel that you've mastered the material, move on to the next part. At the end of your study session, briefly skim through your notes again.

But while review is helpful, cramming last minute is NOT. If at all possible, work ahead so that you won't need to fit all your study into the last day. Cramming overloads your brain with more information than it can process and retain, and your tired mind may struggle to recall even previously learned information when it is overwhelmed with last-minute study. Also, the urgent nature of cramming and the stress placed on your brain contribute to anxiety. You'll be more likely to go to the test feeling unprepared and having trouble thinking clearly.

So don't cram, and don't stay up late before the test, even just to review your notes at a leisurely pace. Your brain needs rest more than it needs to go over the information again. In fact, plan to finish your studies by noon or early afternoon the day before the test. Give your brain the rest of the day to relax or focus on other things, and get a good night's sleep. Then you will be fresh for the test and better able to recall what you've studied.

Step 6: Take a Practice Test

Many courses offer sample tests, either online or in the study materials. This is an excellent resource to check whether you have mastered the material, as well as to prepare for the test format and environment.

Check the test format ahead of time: the number of questions, the type (multiple choice, free response, etc.), and the time limit. Then create a plan for working through them. For example, if you have 30 minutes to take a 60-question test, your limit is 30 seconds per question. Spend less time on the questions you know well so that you can take more time on the difficult ones.

If you have time to take several practice tests, take the first one open book, with no time limit. Work through the questions at your own pace and make sure you fully understand them. Gradually work up to taking a test under test conditions: sit at a desk with all study materials put away and set a timer. Pace yourself to make sure you finish the test with time to spare and go back to check your answers if you have time.

After each test, check your answers. On the questions you missed, be sure you understand why you missed them. Did you misread the question (tests can use tricky wording)? Did you forget the information? Or was it something you hadn't learned? Go back and study any shaky areas that the practice tests reveal.

Taking these tests not only helps with your grade, but also aids in combating test anxiety. If you're already used to the test conditions, you're less likely to worry about it, and working through tests until you're scoring well gives you a confidence boost. Go through the practice tests until you feel comfortable, and then you can go into the test knowing that you're ready for it.

Test Tips

On test day, you should be confident, knowing that you've prepared well and are ready to answer the questions. But aside from preparation, there are several test day strategies you can employ to maximize your performance.

First, as stated before, get a good night's sleep the night before the test (and for several nights before that, if possible). Go into the test with a fresh, alert mind rather than staying up late to study.

Try not to change too much about your normal routine on the day of the test. It's important to eat a nutritious breakfast, but if you normally don't eat breakfast at all, consider eating just a protein bar. If you're a coffee drinker, go ahead and have your normal coffee. Just make sure you time it so that the caffeine doesn't wear off right in the middle of your test. Avoid sugary beverages, and drink enough water to stay hydrated but not so much that you need a restroom break 10 minutes into the test. If your test isn't first thing in the morning, consider going for a walk or doing a light workout before the test to get your blood flowing.

Allow yourself enough time to get ready, and leave for the test with plenty of time to spare so you won't have the anxiety of scrambling to arrive in time. Another reason to be early is to select a good seat. It's helpful to sit away from doors and windows, which can be distracting. Find a good seat, get out your supplies, and settle your mind before the test begins.

When the test begins, start by going over the instructions carefully, even if you already know what to expect. Make sure you avoid any careless mistakes by following the directions.

Then begin working through the questions, pacing yourself as you've practiced. If you're not sure on an answer, don't spend too much time on it, and don't let it shake your confidence. Either skip it and come back later, or eliminate as many wrong answers as possible and guess among the remaining ones. Don't dwell on these questions as you continue—put them out of your mind and focus on what lies ahead.

Be sure to read all of the answer choices, even if you're sure the first one is the right answer. Sometimes you'll find a better one if you keep reading. But don't second-guess yourself if you do immediately know the answer. Your gut instinct is usually right. Don't let test anxiety rob you of the information you know.

If you have time at the end of the test (and if the test format allows), go back and review your answers. Be cautious about changing any, since your first instinct tends to be correct, but make sure you didn't misread any of the questions or accidentally mark the wrong answer choice. Look over any you skipped and make an educated guess.

At the end, leave the test feeling confident. You've done your best, so don't waste time worrying about your performance or wishing you could change anything. Instead, celebrate the successful completion of this test. And finally, use this test to learn how to deal with anxiety even better next time.

Review Video: Test Anxiety
Visit mometrix.com/academy and enter code: 100340

Important Qualification

Not all anxiety is created equal. If your test anxiety is causing major issues in your life beyond the classroom or testing center, or if you are experiencing troubling physical symptoms related to your anxiety, it may be a sign of a serious physiological or psychological condition. If this sounds like your situation, we strongly encourage you to seek professional help.

Online Resources

Due to our efforts to try to keep this book to a manageable length, we've created a link that will give you access to all of your online resources:

mometrix.com/resources719/cqi

It's Your Moment, Let's Celebrate It!

Share your story @mometrixtestpreparation